Weatherproof

Your Home . . . Against the

Storms of Life

Psalm 127:1
Matthew 7

Weatherproof

Your Home . . . Against the

Storms of Life

Doing God's Word—God's Way

Donna Best

REDEMPTION ❘ PRESS

Published by Redemption Press, PO Box 427, Enumclaw, WA 98022

ISBN 13: 978-1-63232-181-7
Library of Congress Catalog Card Number: 2011923323

With all the love in my heart, I dedicate this book to my husband, Larry, the man chosen by God as my life-mate.

Larry has been the greatest support to me in my God-assignment of putting the *Weatherproof* course together and, especially, in writing this book. He has invested in God's work and will reap a harvest to the glory of God.

Contents

PART TWO—OUR FAMILIES

Foreword

Homeland Security Secretary Says Hurricane Could Have "Catastrophic Effects"

THE HEADLINE SHOUTED from the front page of last week's newspaper. People all along America's Gulf coast braced for a major storm, boarding up windows, moving valuables to higher ground, and evacuating under what authorities called a threat of "certain death."

Meanwhile, our small Pennsylvania town was safely sheltered far from the storm's fury. Or so we thought. Although we live a thousand miles from the hurricane's landing point in Texas, its effects brought seventy-miles-per-hour winds with trees crashing into houses, power outages in thousands of homes and workplaces, and disruption to our everyday life for almost a week.

How can we prepare ourselves for the storms of life? How can we weatherproof our homes?

Equally devastating are the storm winds battering our families. Statistics continually reveal the onslaughts wreaking havoc in today's homes. I need look no further than my own circle of friends. Husbands are held captive to pornography and cannot free themselves from its enslaving chains. Wives journey through their daily lives with the questions, "How long until my marriage implodes?" and "Is there any hope?" hovering over them. Sons are taking their own lives or are doing prison time for drugs and theft. Daughters are secretly aborting their unexpected and unwanted babies.

How can we prepare ourselves for the storms of life? How can we weatherproof our homes?

Donna Best has given a wonderful gift to a storm-weary people—a guidebook for weatherproofing our homes against the storms of life. With godly wisdom and refreshing transparency, she provides a study of biblical principles through which God is bringing healing and restoration to women and their families. With strong character but a gentle spirit, she presents "biblical submission as the power of God to produce unity between husbands and wives." And she "demonstrates how the Holy Spirit uses that vital unity to bring about the restoration and preservation of our families."

Best's guidebook originates from neither an unscathed life nor an ivory tower. She has experienced enough storms to be able to say with great conviction, "If God can heal our marriage, He can heal *any* marriage." She has endured many challenges in her own family, emerging with scars of beauty and a passion for God's Word. She has also taught the principles found in this book to women in different parts of this nation, witnessing firsthand the victory that can come when women embrace repentance and biblical submission. God has taken her miseries and transformed them into her ministry.

This book makes no claims to be able to stop the storms of life or their onslaughts to your family. However, it does provide vision of a set-apart people, "visibly holy before the world," and it offers hope to hurting women and their wounded families in the midst of those storms.

Donna Best wonderfully weaves together a simple yet powerful book to point women to wholeness and hope. Read and study it carefully. The result will be a transformation in your heart and home. Then invite a friend to work through it with you. The result will be another transformation in someone else's heart and home.

—**Ken Wilson**
Zelienople, Pennsylvania
(Author of *Finding God in the Bible*,
published by Moody Publishers)

Acknowledgments

WITH DEEP APPRECIATION for the contributions of others in the development of the *Weatherproof* teaching and the completion of this book, I would like to acknowledge and thank:

Ministry advisors: Elise Jefferis, Lynn Marx, and Emma Smith for their untiring support, wise counsel, and unselfish giving of their time to get *Weatherproof Your Home* into the hands of women far and wide.

My friends from Butler, Pennsylvania, who formed a Bible study at Diane Will's home and gave me their enthusiastic encouragement and feedback the first time I taught the *Weatherproof* Bible study. Special thanks to Jill Hanford, who brought it all together.

Barb Johnson, Becky Boros, and Debbie Laslavic, who led *Weatherproof* discussion groups in their homes, giving the book a helpful "test run."

Janet Milo, for encouraging me to broaden the audience from Sunday school to an interdenominational evening study, and for the many other ways she helped promote the class.

The many women (friends!) who served as discussion leaders and team members needed to host the evening classes. Special thanks to Chris Mayti, Jody Eldridge, and Donna Ball for their encouragement and help.

Ken Wilson, who first encouraged me to write the course in the form of a book. From the beginning of this process, he has been a true Godsend in providing guidance and direction.

I saved the best for last. In addition to my husband, Larry, to whom I dedicate this book, I want to thank my wonderful (adult) children. Thanks to my son, Jesse, who was the impetus for change in my life because I love him so much; and to my beloved daughter, Julie, who continually inspires and challenges me to walk in a manner worthy of the Lord, and whose unconditional love for me sustained me through it all.

Suggested *Weatherproof* Bible study format (90 minutes)

THE TWELVE-LESSON *Weatherproof* Bible study is available on DVD through www.donnabest.org. While not necessary for small group discussion of the chapters in this book, the video will enhance your study. Please adapt the material to your situation. Sunday school classes, which typically meet for one hour, may require two weeks to complete each lesson and allow adequate discussion time. In a twelve-week schedule, participants would not meet to discuss Chapter 12. The last class would include discussion of Chapter 11 and viewing of the Lesson 12 DVD. Participants are encouraged to read Chapter 12 on their own after the final class.

Please adjust the following for the first week, which is an introduction to the class, so that the discussion time will be replaced by a time of fellowship, possibly refreshments, and getting to know one another. An ice breaker would be helpful. This would be followed by viewing the DVD for Lesson 1.

10 minutes: Welcome/opening prayer

40 minutes: Small group discussion (Discussion questions are included at the end of each chapter, along with instructions for the facilitator.)

30 minutes: View the DVD teaching. The corresponding book chapter should be read and reflected on individually during the following week in preparation for the next week's discussion.

10 minutes: Closing prayer

Transformation does not occur without reflection. To get the most out of this course:

1. Start a journal where you can respond to the reflection questions presented in each chapter, as well as jotting down anything else the Lord may be showing you.

2. Each chapter includes a memorization verse. It is vitally important that you make the effort to memorize Scripture so that you can replace your thinking with the mind of Christ. To simplify Scripture memorization, visit http://www.Marnie.com to request access to the free online Bible memorization tool.

3. If possible, find an accountability partner from your class with whom you can share confidentially, as you work through the repentance and restoration process.

Introduction

IN THE AFTERWORD of Franklin Graham's autobiography, *Rebel With A Cause,* his parents, Billy and Ruth Graham, included the following statement:

> When Franklin and his buddy, Bill Cristobal, headed for England to pick up the Land Rover to drive to Jordan, Ruth got out her Bible to read John 17 as her prayer for the two boys, and was stopped short at verse nineteen, where she read, "for their sakes, I sanctify myself." If for our sakes the Lord Jesus felt the need to sanctify (dedicate or consecrate) Himself to the Father, how much more did she need to? She put Franklin and Bill "on hold" and set about getting everything straightened out between herself and God.[1]

Mrs. Graham presents a principle that God used in my life to bring healing and restoration to my family, a principle I'll be sharing in the following pages with the hope of bringing that same grace to other families. We "sanctify" ourselves for their sakes. In the Greek, sanctify *(hagiazo)* also means, "to purify internally by renewing of the soul." We can wage spiritual warfare on behalf of our families by dedicating ourselves to the Holy Spirit's process of sanctification, tearing down the strongholds (false beliefs and wrong attitudes) in our own lives, and submitting to God. Before going into battle for our loved ones, we must put on the breastplate of righteousness that Paul tells about in Ephesians 6:14. This not only means we are to stand in the righteousness of Christ that has been credited to us, but also to live it out in our lives.[2]

> Therefore, everyone who hears these words of mine and puts them into practice is like a wise man who built his house on the rock. The rain came down, the streams rose, and the winds blew and beat against that house; yet it did not fall, because it had its foundation on the rock. But everyone who hears these words of mine and does not put them into practice is like a foolish man who built his house on sand. The rain came down, the streams rose, and the winds blew and beat against that house, and it fell with great crash.
> —Matt. 7:24-27

I had always blamed my husband for any family or marriage problems we had, but the Lord spoke to my heart at a critical time in my life, telling me some hard truths about myself. As the Lord continued to teach me, He led me to Ephesians chapter 5. With fresh insight, I saw that the husband is to love his wife as Christ loves the church and gave His life for her. I liked that part! However, God more or less told me to mind my own business and leave my husband to Him. I needed to focus on my responsibilities as a wife. Just as Christ is to be the first love of the church, my husband is to be my first love. I am to treat him with respect, support him in his position of authority over the family, and be devoted to him with all my heart. What a concept! The only problem was that, at the time, we could not stand each other. I had to rely completely on the Holy Spirit to teach me how to do these things and give me the power to do them.

The change didn't happen overnight. In fact, it took almost five years, and it continued to be difficult. Allowing Larry to lead our family went so completely against my nature that I felt the Lord demanded more than I could bear. Yet during that time, I experienced Jesus in a more intimate, tender, and powerful way than I had ever known before. A situation arose that could have brought financial ruin to our family but the Lord impressed on me that He had given my husband the responsibility of resolving the issue. The Lord was calling me to trust Him to work through my husband on my behalf. Feeling frustrated and panicky, I threw myself face down on my bed and cried out, "Lord, I'm so scared!" At that moment, I sensed His presence just as though He was physically leaning over me, and He spoke to my inner being, "I will take care of you." I cannot convey to you the peace and assurance I experienced.

Years later, in August of 2001, I was studying to teach a women's Bible study. My husband (yes, the same one) suggested I put together a course that I could use again, instead of preparing a new Bible study for each class. The Lord had taught me a few things through the years, but I had no idea how to tie them together in a meaningful way. I asked the Lord to show me what He wanted, and soon after, the twelve lesson outlines came easily together. *Weatherproof your Home . . . Against the Storms of Life* is that women's Bible study. The biblical principles taught in this course will speak to women of all ages, from teenagers to grandmothers, to those who want to prepare for their future families or undo the damage of the past.

Contained in these pages is a message of hope and healing as God moves to restore families within the body of Christ. For the most part, Christian families today look no different from non-Christian families. The divorce rate is the same, our children are broken, and addictions are rampant. We have become cultural Christians, adopting the ways of our culture instead of transforming it. We have not built our homes on the Rock; we have not put Christ's words into practice. With the terror attacks of September 11, as well as the events of the past decade, the significance of the title became very clear. The Lord has been sounding an alarm in the body of Christ, warning us that severe storms are coming into our world and into our lives. In order to withstand these storms, we will not only need to know the Word of God, we will also need to put it into practice. We must be fully committed to the repentance and restoration process, which is accomplished as we rely on the power and leading of the Holy Spirit. Then, as the world experiences ever worsening turmoil, many will look at the stability of our lives—a stability they cannot comprehend—and want what we have.

Part One

Our Lives

Chapter 1

The Lives We Construct

I CAN RECALL a day as a new believer when I meditated on Psalm 1, turning the words over in my mind.

> Blessed is the man who does not walk in the counsel of the wicked or stand in the way of sinners or sit in the seat of mockers. But his delight is in the law of the Lord, and on his law he meditates day and night. He is like a tree planted by streams of water, which yields its fruit in season and whose leaf does not wither. Whatever he does prospers.
>
> —Ps. 1:1-3

Sitting in my living room with my Bible on my lap, I began to picture a tranquil scene with a lush tree planted by a quietly flowing stream. Suddenly, the scene changed. A gnarly old tree growing on a river bank leaned precariously over a raging river, as rain and wind pressed hard against it. I realized that God was revealing something He wanted me to understand. He showed me a "cutaway" of the ground underneath the tree. Like an ant farm with all the tunnels underground, the root system of this old tree spread deep and wide into the soil beneath it, giving stability to the trunk of the tree.

The Lord spoke to my heart. He told me that one day I would be like that gnarly old tree: so deeply rooted and grounded in the Word of God that I would not be moved by the storms of life. At the age of

1

'eing old and gnarly was not particularly
·o the Lord, "I don't want to be strong; I
' was facing divorce and pregnant with
⸱ 1977.
⸱ and I did not go through with the divorce,
⸱nd devoted relationship I longed for did not
⸵periodic truces. Perhaps our problems would not have
⸵ to family and friends, but I made sure they knew how I
⸵My childhood had been full of anger, conflict, and alcoholism,
⸱ came away with a victim mentality, which means I had become a
pro" at justifying and excusing my own behavior while blaming others
for everything that was wrong in my life. I gave my life to Christ when
I was twenty-five years old but continued to live this way because I did
not see the truth about myself. I thought that if everyone else in my life
would "straighten up and fly right," my life would be just fine. Instead,
it continued to be full of anger and conflict.

Years later, when we found out our teenage son had been using drugs
(I say this with his permission), I just could not go on as I had. Broken
over my hostile relationship with my husband and the rebellion of our
teenage children, I became willing to do whatever God required to make
things right. The Lord impressed upon me that if I would lay down my
will in obedience to His design for marriage, He would bring peace to
my family for generations. He gave me a verse to hold on to, a picture
of restoration: "All your sons will be taught by the Lord and great will
be your children's peace" (Isa. 54:13). Woven throughout the coming
chapters will be the story of how God restored my marriage and family.

Scripture has much to say about houses: "By wisdom a house is
built, and through understanding it is established; through knowledge
its rooms are filled with rare and beautiful treasures" (Prov. 24:3-4). The
NIV Study Bible comments on the word *house*, as used in this verse,
as "symbolic of the life of an individual or a family."[1] Since individuals
make up the fabric of the family, it is no surprise that in order for God
to restore families, He must first change individuals. He must bring us
to repentance.

In Psalm 127:1 we read, "Unless the Lord builds the house, its
builders labor in vain." Our lives are like houses we build, and that

construction begins in childhood—one choice, one response at a time. As children, we are said to be egocentric, which means we believe the world revolves around us. This is the beginning of the self-centered life.

All of us are aware that children have basic needs beyond food and shelter. Children desperately need nurturing, acceptance, and love, and they need a stable environment where they feel safe. Unfortunately, if children do not have these things, they will react in fear, and that fear will destroy their ability to trust. They may not be able to verbalize it, but their attitude will be, "If I don't take care of myself, no one else will." Fear of not having their needs met can produce an exaggerated sense of self-preservation, compelling children to survive any way they can as they begin to manipulate and control their environment.

The self-reliant life

All sin is meeting our own needs in our own way, independently of God.[2] We'd like to believe that when we come to faith in Christ, we automatically give up that self-centered, self-reliant life, but I don't see that happening. As Christians, we have trusted Christ for salvation but many of us don't trust anyone else to take care of us, and though we may not realize it, our distrust of others often includes God.

We struggle to preserve a life that is not worth preserving. The Lord has not built it—we have.

Our struggle to preserve the life we have built causes us to manipulate and control our circumstances and other people, instead of surrendering control to God. Control is not about having structure and order in our lives. Control, rather, is about *forcing our will* on others in order to have our own way and manipulating our circumstances to produce outcomes we think are best. After all, we reason, we know what's best, don't we? And we only want to help, right? It does not occur to us that we have no right to control others. What's wrong with us? Why can't we let go? I had a compulsive need to tell my husband what he should do and when he should do it, and to control my older children's choices in the same way. I realize now that I thought my survival was at stake, and the driving force in my life was fear.

When I came to faith in Christ, I surrendered my life to Him as best I knew how. In reality, I didn't even know what that meant or what it looked like. Nevertheless, my Savior took me in a "come-as-you-are" condition. Even though I was full of bitterness, He continued to protect me in love and speak to me through His Word over the years. He will never give up on you either. God is in the process of bringing all believers to the end of ourselves, tearing down the lives we've built. In His mercy, God allows enough pain and failure in our lives to enable us to let go of control.

Whom do you trust?

Alcoholism in my birth family took a solemn toll on me and my brothers. Tragically, my youngest brother took his own life at the age of twenty-six. His death has turned out to be, without a doubt, the most traumatic event of my life. Sometime afterward, I went on a long walk, praying for comfort along the way. I said to the Lord, "I know You are trustworthy but there is something very wrong with me, because I can't trust You." I realized that I was powerless to change that, and in desperation, I asked Him to produce that trust in me. How simple! But I first had to see my need; I had to be honest with myself and with God.

Proverbs 3:5-6 was the first Bible passage I memorized as a new believer: "Trust in the Lord with all your heart and lean not on your own understanding; in all your ways acknowledge him, and he will make your paths straight." The Hebrew word for *trust* in this passage is *batach*. It means "to trust; to have confidence in; to be bold; secure; to feel safe, be carefree." When learning this passage, I assumed that I knew what the word *trust* meant. However, the Hebrew meaning suggests a complete trust that enables us to get our eyes off our inadequacies. For many of us, that is our greatest struggle. Yet there is a deeper level of trust we must move toward, and that is to live a bold and fearless life, carefree in the knowledge of His care for us.

Our "own understanding" is our human reasoning, which must be rejected as an unreliable source of truth. Why? Because sin warps our perception of reality. In their pride, the Pharisees insisted on maintaining an idealized view of themselves and could not receive correction when Jesus provided it. According to their human reasoning, they could do no wrong. In Hebrew, to "acknowledge" (*yada*) means, "to know, learn to know; to know by experience." If we are to know God by *experience*, then we will have to walk in His ways because He is not going to walk in ours. I first memorized this passage in the King James Version, which uses the phrase, "He shall direct thy paths." The New International Version states it this way: "He will make your paths straight." I asked the Lord, "What do You mean when You say You'll make my paths straight?" Immediately, the thought came to my mind, "the shortest distance between two points is a straight line." What a great answer! I should be surprised? Perhaps the Lord is telling us that if we will walk with Him (walk in His ways), He'll take us the shortest distance between where we are and where He wants us to be—our destiny in Christ.

How long did the Israelites wander in the desert? Forty years. That was not the shortest distance between two points! I had "wandered in the desert" for twenty years of my Christian life before I awoke to the realization that my life was falling apart because I had done things "my way." I had relied on my human reasoning to protect and preserve my life, rather than relying on God and seeking His ways. *The house we build is the self-centered life based on our own human reasoning.*

The combination of being self-centered and relying on our own human reasoning produces self-reliance. Often, as children, we become self-reliant out of necessity. However, not having our needs met in childhood isn't the only reason we move in that direction. We may become self-reliant simply because we want our own way, and depending on ourselves is the best way to get it. Isaiah refers to this independence as turning to our own ways: "We all, like sheep, have gone astray, each of us has turned to his own way; and the Lord has laid upon him the iniquity of us all" (Isa. 53:6).

We see, then, that even the well-adjusted person who grew up in a loving and nurturing environment is still self-centered from birth. None of us escapes; that is the nature with which we were born. Many years ago, I read a book that included a chapter entitled, "The Perils of the Well-Adjusted."[3] Well-adjusted people are highly functional individuals who "have all their ducks in a row" and do not see their need to change. They don't realize, even after coming to faith in Christ, that they are living self-centered lives based on human reasoning, rather than relying on the Lord. They don't have the same advantage as those of us who have made such a mess of our lives that there's nothing left to do but admit it. However, as Scripture tells us, we *all* have gone astray and God is at work bringing every believer to the realization that the self-centered life we have constructed from childhood has to come down. It is a condemned building, a worthless shack. The Lord will not remodel it; He will tear it down.

God is not in the remodeling business

God will not patch up our "flesh" (a believer's ego, will, and appetites functioning independently of God)[4] to make it look good or function better. He will not repair the life we continued to build on, even after coming to faith in Christ. Instead, His intention for us is that we forsake the self-centered life and turn toward the life He seeks to build for us. That journey toward the God-constructed life is a pilgrimage:

> Blessed are those whose strength is in You, who have set their hearts on pilgrimage. As they pass through the Valley of Baca [weeping], they make it a place of springs; the autumn rains also cover it with pools [blessings]. They go from strength to strength, till each appears before God in Zion. Hear my prayer, O Lord God Almighty; listen to me, O God of Jacob. Look upon our shield, O God; look with favor on your anointed one. Better is one day in Your courts than a thousand elsewhere; I would rather be a doorkeeper in the house of my God than dwell in the tents of the wicked.
> —Ps. 84:5-10, amplification added

A pilgrimage is "a journey to a sacred place."[5] In this case, it is a journey toward a life that is fully surrendered to the will and purposes of God. Though imperfect, the pilgrim has made a *conscious* decision to reject the self-centered life and cooperate with God; he has chosen a God-centered life. This is not a superficial decision based on the emotion of the moment. Instead, it is prompted by brokenness. Some may say that this happens at salvation and we were not truly saved before this time. However, coming to the end of ourselves is part of the sanctification process that begins when we come to faith in Christ. Finding that all my best efforts at living the Christian life had failed, that my problem was indeed me, my only hope was that Christ would change me from the inside out. *The surrendered life that I had feared and fought against had become my deliverance.*

There's something about reaching our forties (mid-life) that encourages surrender. I think it's the physical and emotional exhaustion that comes from trying to orchestrate our lives. By that time, my life had become so painful that I could not function. Crippled by a deep depression, I actually saved up pain pills because the only words that displayed like a banner across the blackness of my mind were "no way out." I sat in my recliner for the better part of two days, not able or caring to shower and go to work. I simply could not go on as I had. That recliner became an altar, and I laid myself upon it, finally becoming willing to face the truth about myself at any cost.

Then I heard God speak gentle rebukes to my heart. He told me that I was the common denominator in all of my conflicts. He also told me that my perception of reality was warped. Oh, yes, and one more thing: He told me that no one can interfere with His will for my life except me, and I had been doing that all my life. I felt as though a murderous enemy had chased me to the edge of a precipice, and down below were the everlasting arms of God—the *Father*. What a dilemma! I had many misconceptions about God the Father that stemmed from my childhood, causing fear and mistrust of Him. Jesus said, "Anyone who has seen Me, has seen the Father" (John 14:9), but I seemed to have missed that part. So, in loving kindness, my heavenly Father brought me to a point of despair, where I had no real choice but to cast myself upon Him in utter abandonment. Do you see His love in all of this? He did for me what I could not do for myself. In the following chapters, I'll be sharing with you the process that the Lord led me through, with the hope that you will experience the same healing and freedom that the Lord has brought about in my own life.

The lives we build are based on wrong beliefs about God

We have two images of God:

- What we know to be true about God, based on His Word
- What we *feel* about God, based on our experiences

It is common for us to assign the characteristics of our earthly fathers to God the Father. If our fathers were harsh, hard, critical, and demanding, we may adopt that view of God. The Lord, however, will lovingly bring us to a place in our lives in which we have no choice but to surrender control to Him. For me, it felt as though I had fallen into a feathered nest (Psalm 91:4). In some miraculous way, the Father began to teach me to trust Him by enabling me to wait on Him to resolve my problems, rather than taking matters into my own hands. That became my point of repentance from my self-reliance to God-dependence, from self-centeredness to God-centeredness.

Tearing down strongholds

This was to be my first experience of tearing down a *stronghold*, in this case a false belief about God the Father. The apostle Paul tells us in Second Corinthians 10:3-5:

> For though we live in the world, we do not wage war as the world does. The weapons of our warfare are not the weapons of the world. On the contrary, they have divine power to demolish strongholds. We demolish arguments and every pretension that sets itself up against the knowledge of God, and we take captive every thought to make it obedient to Christ.

Paul is using warfare language here because we are in a battle for our minds. The following definition will be very helpful to you as you read the remaining chapters: *A stronghold is a strongly held belief or attitude that is contrary to the truth of God's Word, which Satan uses to enslave us to sin.*

Satan has no authority over believers, but if he can deceive us into believing his lies, he can lead us into habitual sin and addictions. The Lord had told me I had a warped perception of reality. When our perception is "warped," it is much like a fun house mirror. It distorts our view, not only of ourselves but of God and the world around us. Our perception becomes warped, first, by those sins committed against us, and then by our own sins. If a male authority figure mistreated us as children, that sin certainly distorts our perception of God.

We need to understand that a stronghold is a false belief or wrong attitude that resides deep within us. It forms our perception, the lens through which we view life. Often, we reject the truth because it doesn't fit our *perception* of the truth. We can read the Word of God and give mental assent, but it may not get down into our hearts because it doesn't get past the filter of our perception. Have you wondered why it is so difficult to live out what you are learning from God's Word? You've probably heard that phrase, "those old tapes are playing." Well, they are! It is as though the lies you have believed are on one side of your mind and the truth of God's Word is on the other. Scripture tells us "a double-minded man is unstable in all his ways" (James 1:8, KJV). If you're living out your life based on the lies you have believed, while at the same time making every effort to apply the truth of God's Word, then your thinking, emotions, and behavior will be very unstable. I know because that's how I lived most of my Christian life.

Instead, we are to be transformed by the renewing of our minds (Romans 12:2). How does that happen? Our false beliefs and wrong attitudes must be recognized and rejected in order to deeply and profoundly embrace the truth of God's Word. We must "take captive every thought to make it obedient to Christ" (2 Cor. 10:5). I had to recognize that my belief about God (that I could not rely on Him to take care of me) did not line up with the truth of His Word, and then consciously reject that lie. Only as I did that could I "erase those old tapes" and replace the lies with the truth: "Trust in the Lord with all thine heart and lean not on thine own understanding. In all thy ways acknowledge him, and he will direct thy paths" (Prov. 3:5-6 KJV). We are to identify and reject every thought that does not line up with the truth of God's Word, taking it captive so that the powerful Word of God can replace it, making us single-minded.

Memorizing Scripture is essential to taking our thoughts captive. But you may groan, "I *can't* memorize." I am at a point in my life where I can't even remember what I said five minutes ago and yet the Holy Spirit enables me to memorize Scripture. God speaks to us out of the storehouse of His Word in us. When we memorize it, we own it. Take a verse or passage that speaks to your heart and invest your time and effort in memorizing it. Satan wants us to believe that we can't memorize Scripture because that's the sword of the Spirit, both a defensive and offensive weapon used to defeat him.

Why don't we believe what God says about Himself in His Word?

- We have generational misconceptions (Our parents instill in us their perceptions of God).
- We judge God by our experience ("If God loved me, He wouldn't let me suffer this way").
- We experienced mistreatment by authority figures in our childhoods.
- We received religious training that promoted shame, guilt, and fear.
- We are blinded by our refusal to forgive others.

Sometimes it is difficult for us to step outside of our own experiences in order to view our lives objectively. Regardless of what your experiences have taught you, the truth is: *We have peace with God through Jesus Christ, our Lord!*

> Since we have now been justified by his blood, how much more shall we be saved from God's wrath through him! For if, when we were God's enemies, we were reconciled to him through the death of his Son, how much more, having been reconciled, shall we be saved through his life? Not only is this so, but we also rejoice in God through our Lord Jesus Christ, through whom we now have reconciliation.
> —Rom. 5:9-11

If you recall, Isaiah 53:6 tells us, "the Lord has laid upon Him the iniquity of us all." God the Father laid upon Christ all of His righteous anger over our sin, and the wonderful news is that Christ not only paid for our sins but He also took the Father's wrath over those sins, on our behalf. Therefore, if we have received Christ as our Savior, God the Father is never angry with us. Now, I don't know about you but I grew up with a lot of anger in our household. When I learned that no matter what I do my heavenly Father is never angry with me, I wanted to leap with joy!

In the following chapters, we are going to study the scriptural truth that God makes a distinction between who we are and what we do. He very definitely deals with our behavior, but He does so as a loving Father

(Hebrews 12:5-6). Because of this, even when He is disciplining me for some attitude or sin in my life, I go to my heavenly Father for comfort while I'm going through the discipline process. Now, if all sin is meeting our own needs in our own way,[6] and we are too afraid to turn to the Father, then we will look for comfort in all the wrong places, and the world has a multitude of ways for us to do that.

In the gospel of John we read, "Whoever believes in the Son has eternal life, but whoever rejects the Son will not see life, for God's wrath remains on him" (John 3:36). You see that God's wrath does not remain on us when we believe in Christ because He took the Father's wrath; He took our sin and gave us His righteousness. I must stress that the Lord loves every person. However, if you have not received Christ and His death as payment for your sin, you have not been reconciled with the Father, and His wrath remains on you. I fear that many church members falsely believe they are saved simply because they belong to a church, attend services, do good works, and try to live a moral lifestyle. However, if you have not entered into that one-on-one transaction with Jesus Christ, trusting in Him alone as your Savior, please consider doing so today and receive God's precious gift of eternal life, made available through His grace alone. The good news is this: "For God so loved the world that he gave his one and only Son, that whoever believes in him shall not perish but have eternal life" (John 3:16).

As we surrender our lives to God, forsaking our own ways, God will tear down those strongholds and construct a new life for us that is built on the truth of His Word. I am now in my sixties, and for most of my life, I dragged the past with me. However, it is for freedom that Christ has set us free (Galatians 5:1), and He doesn't want us to be weighed down by the past. Through Jesus Christ, the living Word of God, we can be free!

> Therefore, I urge you brothers, in view of God's mercy, to offer your bodies as living sacrifices, holy and pleasing to God—this is your spiritual act of worship. Do not conform any longer to the pattern of this world, but be transformed by the renewing of your mind. Then you will be able to test and approve what God's will is—his good, pleasing and perfect will.
>
> —Rom. 12:1-2

Reflection questions

1. Do you believe that God the Father is angry with you over your sins? If so, how has that affected your intimacy (closeness and trust) with Him?
2. Where are you today? Living a life you have built—or the one God has chosen for you? Is it a life of truth or deception? Purpose or pretense? Self or surrender to God?

Will you pray with me?

If you now realize that you never personally trusted Jesus Christ for the forgiveness of your sins and the joy of eternal life with Him, you can offer this simple prayer:

"Lord Jesus, I believe that You are the only begotten Son of God, that You are fully God and fully human. I believe that You led a sinless life and that You died on the cross for the sins of the world—including mine. I believe that God the Father, by the power of the Holy Spirit, raised You from the dead and that You will come again to judge the living and the dead. I ask you to forgive me and save me so that I can be reconciled with my heavenly Father, filled with the Holy Spirit, and live with You forever. I receive You as the Lord of my life and the Master of my soul. In Your Name, I pray. Amen."

Memorization verse:

Proverbs 3:5-6, "Trust in the Lord with all your heart and lean not on your own understanding; in all your ways acknowledge him, and he will make your paths straight."

SMALL GROUP DISCUSSION QUESTIONS

Note to discussion leaders: Before proceeding to the discussion questions, it is helpful to begin by asking the women if there was some point in the assigned chapter that they identified with or that was new to them. If time allows, you may also want to discuss the reflection questions listed at the end of the chapter.

1. We always behave in a way that is consistent with what we believe.[7] What does your pattern of behavior over the years reveal about your ability to trust God? Do you see yourself as *self*-reliant or *God*-dependent? What is it about your history that brings you to that conclusion?

2. How does your view of God as Father affect your closeness with Him? What is your relationship with your father? Do you see any parallel in your view of your earthly father and your heavenly Father?

3. Control is one of the hardest things for us to give up. We often deceive ourselves into thinking that we are helping others. How do you define "control"? Do you think you are truly depending on God if you feel the need to "fix" other people or their circumstances?

Chapter 2 ~❧

The Destruction Caused
by Bitterness

IF YOU ARE intent on working through the repentance and restoration process, and I trust you are, you must be willing to deal with any unforgiveness that you may be harboring toward others. I have learned that we are going nowhere in our Christian walk until we do so.

As we begin, I want to focus on our primary relationships in the family: our parents, siblings, husbands (perhaps, an ex-husband?), and our children. In addition to our family relationships, however, we cannot approach the issue of unforgiveness without bringing up the subject of childhood sexual abuse. Statistics tell us that approximately one in four women and one in six men were sexually abused as children. This is a major trauma in a child's life, and God so longs to bring healing to that individual. However, we must understand that forgiveness is critical to the healing process; without it, the effects of abuse will continue.

Jesus told his disciples, "For if you forgive men when they sin against you, your heavenly Father will also forgive your sins. But if you do not forgive men their sins, your Father will not forgive your sins" (Matt. 6:14–15). What is forgiveness? The Greek word for *forgive* is *aphiemi,* which means to "let go; release; cancel a debt." When we withhold forgiveness, it is as though we have our hands around our offenders' throats. We want to wring her neck; we want to make him pay. But God is there, telling us, "No, I'll handle that. 'It is Mine to avenge, I will repay'"

(Rom. 12:19). When we refuse to forgive, we are saying "no" to God. We do not "let go." We do not release our offenders. God then turns us over to our sin, and we reap what we have sown (Gal. 6:7). That means that God will not release us from the *burden of our guilt*. We will drag it around day after day, month after month, and year after year, until we release our offenders to God through forgiveness.

I'd like to take you to what may be for many of you a familiar passage in Scripture. If you have a Bible available, please read the entire account of the parable of the unmerciful servant in Matthew 18:21-35. If not, I will summarize it for you as follows. There are three points in particular which I want to make from this reading:

First, the unmerciful servant (a picture of us) owed his master (God) a huge debt, the equivalent of millions of dollars (more, in today's economy), compared to a few months' wages owed to him by his fellow servant (our offenders).

Second, the unmerciful servant asked for time because he thought he could pay back what he owed to his master, but he had deceived himself about the magnitude of his debt. This is a picture of us, as we deceive ourselves about the magnitude of our sin, and our desperate need for God's mercy. We can't pay the penalty for our own sins.

Third, the unmerciful servant refused to forgive the relatively minor debt owed him by his fellow servant and, instead, had him thrown into prison until he could pay. Initially, the master had forgiven the very large debt of the unmerciful servant. When he learned, however, that this servant had refused to cancel the debt of his fellow servant, the master turned him over to the jailers to be *tortured* until he could pay back all he owed. Jesus then tells us, "This is how my heavenly Father will treat each of you unless you forgive your brother from your heart." (Matt. 18:35).

Yes, that's what Jesus said. For years, I always missed that part. And how did Jesus say the Father (Who loves us) would treat *us* if we do not forgive? He's going to turn us over to be tortured. Let's look at that. To be "turned over to the jailers to be tortured" is a picture of God withholding the fullest extent of His mercy so that we reap what we have sown—until we repent. Obviously, we received God's mercy when we trusted Christ as our Savior and received the gift of eternal life. However, here Jesus' statement refers to reaping what we have sown in the "here and now." We will bring about our own misery until we become willing to forgive. You might think, *Oh, God would never do that.* But Jesus just said that He would! I want to make it clear, though, that God's actions here are not done in anger and they are not punitive (for the sake of punishment only), but rather, redemptive. God uses consequences to bring us to repentance and teach us His ways.

Tortured in mind, will, and emotions

The Greek word for *jailers* is *basanistes.* It means "one who elicits the truth by the use of the rack; an inquisitor, torturer." Bill Gothard, in his teaching *How To Tear Down A Stronghold Of Bitterness,* explains: These "tormentors [are] afflictions allowed by God to teach us mercy."[1] Let's "unpack" this, as we like to say! To "torture" means "to cause pain and toil; to produce anguish and vexation of soul."[2] The soul is a person's mind, will, and emotions. Let's go deeper: "anguish" is defined as "extreme pain, distress, and anxiety."[3] This would include any and all tormenting emotions, including fear, anger, discouragement, depression, worry, and guilt. The very picture of misery, wouldn't you say?

This tells us that it's not what other people have done to us that has the power to take away our peace and joy. It's our refusal to forgive them that produces "anguish of soul." "But the fruit of the Spirit is love, joy, peace, patience, kindness, goodness, faithfulness, gentleness, and self-control" (Gal. 5:22-23). Those are good things to have, are they not? Would you be happy if you were experiencing them? The fruit of the Spirit is actually the very life and virtue of Jesus Christ being produced in us by the indwelling of the Holy Spirit. What a joy to live that life! No one else can take that away from us; that's between us and our Lord.

If we have severe emotional pain in our lives—tormenting emotions—we must always look at unforgiveness as a possible root cause. Depression is among the tormenting emotions listed above, and treatment for it has reached epidemic proportions. There are physiological causes for depression, to be sure. However, the depression for which many are being medicated may very well be caused by the individual's refusal to forgive.

Remember also that if we don't forgive others, we will not experience a release from our own guilt. If we feel guilt and condemnation, even after we have confessed our sin, we need to look at our refusal to forgive others as the possible cause. With the divorce rate over 50 percent, even among Christians, we can see that spouses are blaming each other for their "anguish of soul," when in fact they are reaping the consequences of their own unforgiveness. Do you see how bitterness distorts our perception of reality and deceives us about the real cause of our misery?

I had a habit of complaining about my husband to others, always portraying myself as the innocent victim. (Can you relate?) On one occasion, I happened to be speaking to a young man named Klaus, who attended my church. He and his family were from Germany and had moved here to be trained at a nearby New Tribes Missions school. He had been to our home and had met Larry. I began to tell Klaus about something that Larry had done and what I had to put up with in my marriage. You know what I mean . . . playing the martyr. When I had finished telling him my sad tale, thinking he would feel so sorry for me, he looked at me with all the love in his heart and said: "Donna, your failure to love Larry is as sinful in God's eyes as anything Larry has done."

I was speechless! Yet God poured out His grace on me so that I could receive that "word from the Lord" because I had already asked Him to tear down the stronghold of bitterness in my life. To this day, I love that young man for speaking the truth to me. That one statement has changed my life like no other.

God's purpose in turning us over to the "jailers" is to make us recognize how much mercy we require ("to elicit the truth"). We must face the truth about ourselves. God showed me that I had done more damage to our children by the way I had treated their father (with contempt and disrespect), than he had ever done to them. I realized that I did not have the power to undo the damage. True brokenness comes not as a result of the pain others have caused us, but rather from a revelation of the pain we have caused and the damage we have done to others. If my children were to be healed, God would have to do it. That's when I understood what mercy is: instead of reaping what I had sown all those years, I could reap what Jesus Christ had sown on my behalf, if I would repent (acknowledge my sin and become willing to do whatever God required to make things right).

God's life preserver

Imagine you're drowning in a sea of bitterness and anguish of soul. Why are you drowning? Because you're not swimming, and you're not treading water. You have your hands firmly around your offender's throat. And you're so intent on making that person pay for how he or she has hurt you, that you're oblivious to the fact that you're about to go under for the last time.

I want you to picture a life preserver with the words "God's Mercy" written on it. I found myself in the middle of an emotional breakdown when the Lord showed me a glimpse of His mercy in the form of that life preserver. I realized then that I had a choice to make. In order to lay hold of the mercy of God, I would have to release my husband, the person I had blamed for my misery. Hmmm . . . let me think. Which would I prefer: the mercy of God or anguish of soul? I'll take the mercy of God!

Do not give the devil a foothold

Can you think of a movie you've watched where someone knocks at the door, and the person inside opens the door without asking, "Who's there?" As soon as the person inside realizes that the person at the door intends harm, he or she quickly tries to shut the door. Unfortunately, the intruder wedges his foot in the doorway and the person inside is unable to close the door. In fact, all the intruder needs to do at that point to gain access into the home is to put his weight against the door and push it open. It's too late! The person inside is helpless! This is a picture of us when we give Satan a "foothold" in our lives through unresolved anger.

Let's look at Ephesians 4:26–27 to find out what God has to say about giving Satan access to our lives: "In your anger do not sin. Do not let the sun go down while you are still angry, and do not give the devil a foothold." "Foothold" is defined as "a position usable as a base for further advance."[4] In a battle, it means giving ground to the enemy.

As our enemy, Satan is given control, *not as in possession,* but as in habitual sin or addiction. Satan has no authority over believers because we are in Christ. However, he uses deception to lure us into sin when we don't take God at His Word. Here, we give him legal access to our lives through the sin of unresolved anger, which leads to a "root of bitterness." *Bitterness is prolonged unforgiveness and unresolved anger that lies just beneath the surface.*

We often think we have forgiven, but the issue continues to surface. It's like mowing down a dandelion, only to have it "pop up" again because we did not destroy the root. From my early childhood, I learned to respond to offenses through *unforgiveness.* I didn't know how to forgive. I thought it meant "sweeping things under the rug," suppressing my anger and pain. Over time, bitterness takes root and we can't untangle ourselves from it. Bitterness becomes an addiction, a habitual sin we can't break. It warps our perception of reality, producing a victim mentality and self-pity. At that point, only God can deliver us from our dilemma.

Bitterness is a *stronghold* because it is an attitude toward others that is contrary to God's Word and gives Satan "a position usable as a base for further advance,"[5] which means he is able to use it to enslave us to sin. We will be looking at "generational strongholds" in Chapter 9, and this is an example of one. Holding grudges and withholding forgiveness can be a sin that is modeled and passed on from one generation to the next. Here's a frightening thought: If we do not forgive our parents, our children will not forgive us. That's what it means to reap what we have sown. We must also realize that we will train our own children to become bitter if we do not repent. The cycle will go on and on unless we become willing to practice forgiveness.

I want to say more on the subject of addiction and its relationship to bitterness. There is so much addiction within the church. We see individuals struggling with all kinds of problems: pornography, food abuses, drug and alcohol abuse, sexual addictions, child abuse, and, now, the misuse of prescription medications. These abuses, too, occur within the whole spectrum of the Christian family—parents and children alike. Oftentimes, we focus on alleviating the symptoms, but the Lord has taught me to go to the root of the problem. I've learned that rebellion will get you into an addiction, but *bitterness will keep you there.* Why?

At the heart of bitterness is pride: we are self-righteous and don't see the depths of our own sin or our need for mercy. James 4:6b tells us, "God opposes the proud but gives grace to the humble." So we see here that until we humble ourselves and become willing to forgive, we cannot receive the grace we need to get free from our addictions. Once we have given the devil a foothold, only God can close the door and set us free.

Symptoms of bitterness include sarcasm (I thought of sarcasm as my "sense of humor"); contempt (am I the only one who has spoken contemptuously to her husband?); withholding our affections from our offenders (cold shoulder: "Oh, I'm not angry with him; I just don't want to talk to him); and the desire to "get even" (retaliating). How about replaying those mental tapes? Do you find yourself reliving an offense in your mind and then telling others what your offender has done? Each time we do, we convince ourselves even more that we are justified in our unresolved anger and resentment. Yet we neglect to see that according to God's Word, we are not.

Defilement of the soul

Have you ever experienced a computer virus? It's not that I would wish it on you, but for the purpose of this analogy, it would be helpful! I asked the Lord to give me a picture of what happens to us through unforgiveness, but before I share that with you, let's look at Hebrews 12:14–15: "Make every effort to live in peace with all men and to be holy; without holiness no one will see the Lord. See to it that no one misses the grace of God and that no bitter root grows up to cause trouble and defile many." There's that bitter root again! I had to look up the word *defile* in the dictionary, since it isn't a word commonly used today. It means "to corrupt or to make filthy."[6] When I asked the Lord to give me a word picture, He brought to my mind a computer virus I had experienced. I've learned that once a virus corrupts one file, it spreads to every file in your computer until eventually it shuts you down.

That's a picture of bitterness. You may have someone in your past (perhaps a parent or a person who violated you sexually as a child or it may be your husband today, with ongoing offenses) and you think you can just harbor unforgiveness toward that one individual, but you will love everyone else "with the love of the Lord." However, your soul (mind, will, and emotions) becomes corrupted by that bitterness and soon it affects every other relationship you have. In time, you will become a bitter person.

Another analogy we can use here is seeing ourselves as a container, perhaps a lovely vase, filled up to our necks with the debris (filth) of bitterness. How much capacity does that leave us to love God? Not much. *Bitterness diminishes our capacity to love God.* So many of us think we love God, but we have no idea how much we *could* love Him, if only we would forgive others. What is considered the greatest commandment? "Love the Lord your God with all your heart and with all your soul and with all your mind and with all your strength" (Mark 12:30). This is the greatest commandment and bitterness renders us incapable of obeying it. Then, because our obedience in every area of our lives flows out of our love relationship with the Lord, we continually struggle to obey God.

Do you ever get frustrated because you want to obey God, but you fail repeatedly with no real understanding as to why that is? When I had been a Christian for almost twenty years, I asked myself, "Why haven't I changed? Why am I not seeing the fruit of the Spirit in my life?" Because I had become so full of bitterness, I had very little capacity to love God *and experience His love for me*, out of which my obedience would flow.

He restores my soul

When we have given the enemy a "foothold" in our lives through unresolved anger and prolonged unforgiveness, producing a root of bitterness, God alone will be capable of "restoring our souls" (Psalm 23:3). Hosea 5:15 tells us (God is speaking here): "Then I will go back to my place until they admit their guilt. And they will seek my face; in their misery they will earnestly seek me." Do you see the principle playing out here? God allows us to become so miserable that we become willing to repent of our sin. Yes, He wants to deal with our sin, but He also wants to heal us and set us free. So He steps back and lets us have our way until we become so miserable that we earnestly seek Him.

At that point in my own life, I cried out to Him, "Lord, please deal with my sin, the things I can't even face. I have brought all this pain on myself through my own sin. Please forgive me as I willingly forgive all others!"

The twenty-third psalm is a very familiar passage to many of us, but perhaps you have never seen it as it relates to God restoring our souls from the destruction we have brought upon ourselves through unforgiveness. *When we repent, God restores our souls: our minds, our wills, and our emotions.*

Verse 1: "The Lord is my shepherd, I shall not be in want." There's so much more of God's love that we can *experience* when we choose to forgive. God will cleanse us of the filth of bitterness and enable us to receive His love for us.

Verse 2: "He makes me lie down in green pastures; he leads me beside quiet waters. . . ." Christ leads us through the Holy Spirit. Our lives don't have to be one crisis after another because of our wrong decisions.

Verse 3: "He restores my soul. He guides me in paths of righteousness for his name's sake." We can have a clear conscience and peace of mind.

Verse 4: "Even though I walk through the valley of the shadow of death, I will fear no evil, for you are with me; your rod and your staff, they comfort me." We will not be overcome with fear because we can sense His presence. We will no longer be tormented by our emotions.

Verse 5: "You prepare a table before me in the presence of my enemies. You anoint my head with oil; my cup overflows." God will deal with those who hurt us; we can move on to enjoy the abundant life that Christ died to give us. He restores to us what others have taken. He alone can heal us. We forgive out of obedience, but we also forgive because it is the only way to be healed of what others have done to us.

Verse 6: "Surely goodness and love [mercy] will follow me all the days of my life, and I will dwell in the house of the Lord forever." We can experience and enjoy the love of God, and have the capacity to love Him in return (our deepest need). "We love because he first loved us" (1 John 4:19).

Since the Lord has shown me the absolute necessity of forgiving others, I now know what it is to spend intimate time alone with God in that secret place where He is enthroned in me, and I can receive the love He has for me. His love restores my soul so that I am no longer emotionally needy, controlling other people or doing whatever else it takes to get my needs met. I can go before Him and receive everything I need and then pour it out to others. My soul is being healed and restored, and that is what He wants for every one of us.

The process of forgiveness

Forgiveness is a choice we make and then a process we work through, as we surrender control to the Holy Spirit. The past is not truly in the past until we deal with it. If we're still harboring unforgiveness in our hearts, it is today's sin, no matter how long ago the injury occurred. Let's look at what forgiveness is—and what it is not!

It is *not* "sweeping it under the rug" or trying to ignore the pain. Many of us grew up in households where issues and conflicts were not resolved. No one admitted being wrong or apologized for hurting another. You were just supposed to go on as though nothing had happened. That is not forgiveness.

- It is *not* reconciliation—that takes two.
- It is *not* saying it doesn't matter or making excuses for your offender.
- It *is* accepting the reality that what your offender did to you was wrong.
- It *is* releasing the person to God to be dealt with as God sees fit.
- It *is* for *your* good.
- It *is* God's will.
- It *is* a choice!

We will either walk in forgiveness, or we will live in bitterness. We will either choose to forgive, or we will choose to retaliate. Those are our only two options. And we retaliate in different ways.

My recommendation is to begin by asking the Lord to help you make a list of all whom you have not truly forgiven, those toward whom you have negative feelings or from whom you have closed off your affections. It's important to ask the Lord to show you, since you may have blocked out your bitterness towards someone. Include yourself (ways in which you have degraded yourself through sin or injured and failed others, etc.). You may need to include God on your list. He has never wronged you, but you may have become bitter towards Him because of situations He allowed in your life ("Lord, if You love me, how could You let this happen?").

On a sheet of paper, make two columns on which you can list (on the left) the names of those God brings to mind. Under each name, state honestly what that person did that so deeply hurt you. (It really does help to write it down and look at it.) Then, in the right hand column, beside each name, honestly state your sinful response to him or her. How have you retaliated? If you did not forgive, you retaliated—those are our only two options. And I've found that we all retaliate in different ways. Some people are soft-spoken and non-confrontational but may talk about their offenders and slander them behind their backs. We're all guilty of that at times, aren't we? That's what is called passive-aggressive. It's making someone pay in an indirect way. Other ways of retaliating are giving our offenders the cold shoulder or acting angry with them. What is your method of retaliation?

Hold onto this list temporarily, since we will be referring to it in the next chapter.

Reflection questions

1. I must admit that I blamed *all* my unhappiness on my husband. Whom have you blamed for your "anguish of soul"? Try to be as specific as you can as to what destructive emotions you have struggled with and the person you blamed for them.
2. Have you given Satan a foothold in your life by not resolving your anger or not choosing to forgive? Is there habitual sin in your life that may be related to your refusal to forgive?
3. Can you look back over your life and think of times when you made decisions that you were convinced were right, only to find out later were wrong? How did these decisions result in crises for you and/ or your family?

Will you pray with me?

If you are ready and willing for the Lord to set you free from bitterness, simply ask Him:

"Heavenly Father, please do not treat me as my sins deserve but have mercy on me. I confess that I have harbored unforgiveness in my heart, and that I have not walked in love. I realize now that much of my pain resulted from my own sin of unforgiveness, and that I have deceived myself. Only You can change me. I am trusting in You for the ability to show mercy to my offenders and to allow Your Word to transform me. I pray that the life and virtue of Jesus Christ would be made manifest in me, for it is in Christ's Name I pray. Amen."

Memorization verse

Matthew 6:15, "But if you do not forgive men their sins, your Father will not forgive your sins."

SMALL GROUP DISCUSSION QUESTIONS

Note to discussion leaders: Before proceeding to the discussion questions, it is helpful to begin by asking the women if there was some point in the assigned chapter that they identified with or that was new to them. If time allows, you may also want to discuss the reflection questions listed at the end of the chapter.

1. Can you think of a specific example in your life where you struggled to forgive someone? Why do you think it was so difficult for you?
2. Can you see how bitterness has affected your ability to experience God's love for you?
3. Bitterness can be a generational stronghold. As you look back over your past, do you see any pattern in your relationships where you held a grudge? Was there a pattern in your family, or in the family of someone close to you, in which you saw this stronghold? This is not to blame our parents for the bitterness we see in ourselves, but rather to identify the root cause and then reject it.

Chapter 3 〰

Experiencing God's Mercy

IN THE PARABLE of the unmerciful servant, we saw from God's Word that unless we forgive (release our offenders to God), our Father in heaven will not forgive us (release us from the *burden* of our guilt). Mercy, however, goes beyond forgiveness: it is "compassion shown to an offender"[1]; kindness and forgiveness, especially when given to a person who doesn't deserve it, one who, perhaps, isn't even sorry for the pain he's caused. Mercy is treating an offender the opposite of what he or she deserves. Ephesians 2:1-7 is a powerful account of the mercy we have been shown in Christ:

> As for you, you were dead in your transgressions and sins, in which you used to live when you followed the ways of this world and of the ruler of the kingdom of the air, the spirit who is now at work in those who are disobedient. All of us also lived among them at one time, gratifying the cravings of our sinful nature and following its desires and thoughts. Like the rest, we were by nature objects of wrath. But because of his great love for us, God, who is rich in mercy, made us alive with Christ even when we were dead in transgressions—it is by grace you have been saved. And God raised us up with Christ and seated us with him in the heavenly realms in Christ Jesus, in order that in the coming ages he might show the incomparable riches of his grace, expressed in his kindness to us in Christ Jesus.

Is that what we deserve? The apostle Paul, who wrote the above in a letter to the Ephesians, also tells us, "For the wages of sin [what we've earned and deserve] is death, but the gift of God is eternal life in Jesus Christ our Lord" (Rom. 6:23, amplification added). We deserved death: physical death and eternal separation from God. But when we came to faith in Christ, the Father not only forgave our sins. He went so far beyond forgiveness. He placed us into Christ and seated us with Him in the heavenly realms (Ephesians 2:6). And that's also past tense, which is hard to comprehend, but it means that "Christians live in two realities at the same time: their physical world and in the heavenlies in Christ."[2] I can't see you (or me) seated with Christ in the heavenly realms, so how do I know it's true? Because God's Word tells us it is! That's what it means to walk by faith and not by sight. We are to believe and live out our lives based on what God's Word states is true of us, not by what we think or how we feel, nor by outward appearances. *Receiving God's mercy means that instead of reaping what we have sown, we reap what Jesus Christ has sown on our behalf.*

However, and this is a big "however," we cannot *experience* God's mercy until we become willing to extend it to others (Matthew 6:15). Galatians 6:7 tells us: "Do not be deceived: God cannot be mocked. A man reaps what he sows." We've already seen that because of our faith in Christ, we have not reaped what we have sown in the eternal, spiritual realm. If you've trusted in Christ as your Savior, you've already had *all* of your sins (past, present, and future) forgiven at the moment of your salvation. That's the spiritual (eternal) reality.

It is in this physical realm—the "here and now"—that we reap what we sow. God uses consequences (reaping) to bring us to repentance and teach us His ways (a lifelong process). If we do not forgive others, God will not *release* us from the burden of our guilt. We will carry our guilt around day after day, month after month, year after year. When the burden becomes so great that we can't bear it any longer, God asks us if we are ready to forgive our offenders, and we can answer, "Yes, Lord."

Liar, liar!

Forgiveness is an aspect of love. "Love. . . . keeps no record of wrongs" (1 Cor. 13:4-5). For most of my life, until I learned what I am sharing here, I believed that my greatest need was to be loved. The world tells us that if the right person loves us in the right way, we will be blissfully happy. That is a lie that encourages people to exchange one spouse for another on a never-ending search for that "right" person. However, the Bible tells us that God Himself has loved us with a perfect love. The Lord showed me, instead, that my greatest need is the *capacity to love others*. I did not have it; bitterness had filled my soul.

"We love because He first loved us. If anyone says, 'I love God,' yet hates his brother, he is a liar. For anyone who does not love his brother, whom he has seen, cannot love God, whom he has not seen" (1 John 4:19-20). I know that if you're anything like me, you'll go right to the word *hate* and say, "I don't hate anyone." Yet, if you'll notice in the next line, it says, "anyone who does not love." In God's eyes, not loving is the same as hating. I had to look at that second verse and realize that if I didn't love my husband, whom I have seen, I could not love God Whom I have not seen. How often had I read that verse before? Like the Pharisees, those self-righteous religious leaders of Jesus' day, I knew what God's Word said but I did not apply it to myself. I had to get completely honest with God and tell Him, "Lord, I'm a liar and I don't love You." Isn't that the truth? If I didn't love my husband, it demonstrated that I didn't truly love God and was a liar for saying that I did. What was my recourse? A simple prayer: "Father, please enable me to love Larry with all of my heart and be devoted to him until the day I die."

That kind of surrender, laying down my fears, insecurities, and desires, seemed so scary to me. Because of the pain of my past, I had never given Larry my *whole* heart. However, God began setting me free to love wholeheartedly and with abandon.

How can we experience God's mercy?

As we become willing to extend mercy to our offenders, we need to recognize what is necessary for true repentance. Let's look at James 1:22-25:

> Do not merely listen to the word, and so deceive yourselves. Do what it says. Anyone who listens to the word but does not do what it says is like a man who looks at his face in a mirror and, after looking at

himself, goes away and immediately forgets what he looks like. But the man who looks intently into the perfect law that gives freedom, and continues to do this, not forgetting what he has heard, but doing it—he will be blessed in what he does.

Remember what I said about having read the Word, but not applying it to myself? James tells us we deceive ourselves when we do that. When we operate out of our "flesh," we seek to maintain an idealized view of ourselves, just as the Pharisees did. Instead, we must apply the Word of God to ourselves in order to tear down those false beliefs and wrong attitudes that we call strongholds, in this case, a stronghold of bitterness.

There is no other option given us in Scripture except to release our offenders to God. Many will say, "I have a right to be angry." You may have, but you were to relinquish that right before the sun went down: "In your anger do not sin: Do not let the sun go down while you are still angry, and do not give the devil a foothold" (Eph. 4:26-27). Others may say, "When they come to me to apologize, then I'll forgive." *We are not to make excuses or justify our bitterness.* We are to forgive even if our offenders never acknowledge what they have done. As Jesus hung on the cross, He said, "Father, forgive them for they do not know what they are doing" (Luke 23:34). Mercy is forgiveness and kindness shown to a person who doesn't deserve it.

We have seen through Scripture that when we refuse to forgive, God turns us over to tormenting emotions, and that is the reason for our anguish of soul (Matthew 18:34-35). We are reaping what we have sown; we have brought this pain on ourselves. *We are not to blame anyone else for our anguish of soul.* Taking responsibility for the pain in our lives is so powerful. As long as we believe that someone else is to blame for what's going on inside of us, there's not a thing we can do to remove the pain. However, if we take responsibility, we can choose to change, and our lives will change!

Pray for a revelation of your sin. We hear a lot about "brokenness" in Christian circles, as it relates to the painful experiences in our lives. I've found, however, that true brokenness is "a broken and contrite heart" (Psalm 51:17). It is not a result of the pain others have caused us, but rather comes from a realization of the pain we have caused and the damage we have done. *We must recognize our desperate need for God's mercy.* I will speak of myself: I saw myself as innocent and had no real revelation of my sin of refusing to love and forgive. Do you recall, from Chapter 2, the words Klaus spoke to me?

"Donna, your failure to love Larry is as sinful in God's eyes as anything Larry has done."

May I say that it takes more love to tell people the truth than it does to tell them what they want to hear? It's very risky business! We can make it very unpleasant for anyone who tries to confront us concerning the sin in our lives, can't we?

Make a conscious decision to release your offender to God

Next, we must make a conscious decision to release our offenders to God, and allow Him to deal with them as He sees fit. Just imagine yourself releasing your grip from around your offender's throat. Only then can our hands be lifted up to receive the emotional healing that the Lord longs to bring about in our lives. Let's look at Luke 6:32-36 for a better understanding:

> If you love those who love you, what credit is that to you? Even "sinners" love those who love them. And if you do good to those who are good to you, what credit is that to you? Even "sinners" do that. And if you lend to those from whom you expect repayment, what credit is that to you? Even "sinners" lend to "sinners," expecting to be repaid in full. But love your enemies, do good to them, and lend to them without expecting to get anything back. Then your reward will be great, and you will be sons of the Most High, because he is kind to the ungrateful and wicked. Be merciful, just as your Father is merciful.

Have any enemies? I'm convinced that you do, just as I do, based on the biblical meaning of the word (*echthros*), which is "hostile, hating; and opposing another." Can you think of anyone who opposes you? It may be a member of your own family, one who puts you down and continually finds fault with you. In fact, it could even be a parent. Yet we are called to do good to our enemies and be merciful to them. I know that is a very tall order.

Think about the Ephesians passage I used at the beginning of this chapter to point out the mercy of God shown to us in Christ (Ephesians 2:1-7). Note that this passage is past tense: "We *were* by nature objects of wrath" (v. 3). If you recall, in Chapter 1, I made the point that if you have come to faith in Christ, you have been reconciled with God the Father and Christ took upon Himself all the Father's wrath (righteous anger) caused by your sins. Did you take note of how merciful your heavenly Father is? What God has planned for us, totally in His mercy and grace, is beyond our comprehension. In order to be like our Father in heaven, we must become willing to extend mercy to our offenders.

Making amends

You are at the point now where you must be willing to extend mercy to your offender in *tangible ways*. To be honest, you may not be willing—but be willing to be made willing! God will help you where you are. This leads us to making amends. Please note: Do not take any steps to make amends until you have read this chapter in its entirety. This is a process, one that should be entered into carefully and prayerfully.

Making amends has been a very humbling experience for me, yet I would not exchange it for anything because of the awesome "harvest" it produced in me and in my relationships. Proverbs 28:13 tells us, "He who conceals his sins does not prosper, but he who confesses and renounces them finds mercy." I openly had to acknowledge my sin, not simply confess it in my heart. I had to repair the damage I had done, in whatever way God led me to do that.

"Fools mock at making amends for sin, but goodwill is found among the upright" (Prov. 14:9). Making amends means taking responsibility for what we've done wrong and then making restitution. Restitution means to restore the loss or repair the damage we have done. We can't always do that, but there is much we can do, and the Holy Spirit will show us what that is. I've already told you that I showed contempt and disrespect for my husband—in front of our children. The Lord showed me I had done more damage to our children by the way I had treated their father than my husband had by anything he had done.

Remember, true repentance means we become willing to do whatever God requires to make things right. The Lord required me to go to my husband and ask for his forgiveness, but I also had to repair the damage. And the way I had to do that (and you must let the Holy Spirit lead you in this) was to go to my children and confess to them that I had been totally wrong all those years for disrespecting their dad. Would they please forgive me, as well, for the way I had damaged them and modeled the wrong attitude for them? That was very humbling but brought tremendous healing to my children.

Let's proceed to Luke 6:41–42, which tells us:

> Why do you look at the speck of sawdust in your brother's eye and pay no attention to the plank in your own eye? How can you say to your brother, "Brother, let me take the speck out of your eye," when you yourself fail to see the plank in your own eye? You hypocrite, first take the plank out of your own eye, and then you will see clearly to remove the speck from your brother's eye.

I want to focus here on verse 42: "you yourself fail to see the plank in your own eye." I found that the King James Version uses the word *perceive* instead of *see*. If you recall, I told you that God showed me that my "perception of reality was warped." Let me tell you, if we have a plank—a large wooden beam—protruding from one eye (and it's been there so long that we have eyelashes growing all around it), our perception of reality is warped. We are blind in one eye and have no peripheral vision in the other. This plank of judgment is so long that it keeps us at a distance from others, but isn't it odd how we can still see a speck in their eyes while oblivious to the huge plank sticking out of ours?

Then it goes on to state, "You hypocrite." (Jesus could be very confrontational at times, couldn't He? He certainly didn't seek approval from people.) In the Greek *(hupokrites)*, hypocrite means "actor, pretender." What do we pretend? We pretend that we are innocent and everyone else is to blame. "All a man's ways seem innocent to him" (Prov. 16:2). "First, take the plank out of your own eye. . . ." In the Greek, the phrase *take out (ekballo)* means "to cast out." It is the same phrase used when Jesus cast the money changers out of the temple (Matthew 21:12), and He did that with force, didn't He? So this is something we have to do forcefully; it is not something that will happen on its own. It implies we will have to take action.

I know that when I read this verse in the past, I interpreted it to mean, "acknowledge your sin." I certainly could admit that I have sinned, but that's not what it is saying here. It means take it out by force. I have found that the most effective way to take that plank of judgment out of my eye is by making amends to others for the wrongs I have done. When we make amends, we take responsibility, we make restitution, and we make things right.

Don't just acknowledge you have a plank in your eye . . . take it out by making amends.

If you are truly repentant, you will do whatever God requires to make things right because you hate your sin more than you love your pride and ego. Making amends also destroys a root of bitterness because it humbles us and God gives grace to the humble (James 4:6). Take responsibility for your sinful reaction to your offender.[3] In the assignment from Chapter 2, as you began the process of forgiveness, I asked you to make two columns on a sheet of paper. In the left column, you were to list those offenders who came to your mind and how they had hurt you. In the right column, you were to note how you had retaliated or reacted to them in a sinful manner.

First, you have to choose to forgive them, then humble yourself, go to each of them, and ask for forgiveness for the way you've treated them. You may think some of them have been "95 percent wrong" and you were only "5 percent wrong," but God is dealing with *you.* Isolate your behavior and take an honest look at it. Was it right or was it wrong? If it was wrong, you need to ask for forgiveness. You are not to go to your offender to bring up his offense *at this time,* but allow God to work in his heart. The Lord can soften his heart through your humility and lack of accusation. You go only to acknowledge what you've done wrong, and you humbly keep silent even if he does not respond graciously to your apology. Why do this? Have you ever decided to "straighten things out" with someone, and said to him, "Well, I did this, but you did that." He immediately went on the defensive and you ended up in a huge argument!

I mentioned before that I had to go to my husband and children to make amends, but my immediate family members were not the only ones I needed to approach. I had to respond to the Holy Spirit's prompting to go to specific people in my life, some from my past whom He required me to seek out. Some had offended me and I had retaliated (reacted sinfully), while others were completely innocent.

When I was nineteen years old and looking for a job, a friend's father hired me and helped me in many ways. Unfortunately, at that time, I did not show him appreciation for all he had done. Twenty years had passed since then, but I wanted to make things right. He had since retired, but I found his phone number and went to visit him and his wife. When I told them I was there to apologize for my lack of appreciation, they were both surprised and so gracious.

Not every instance has been that pleasant. Others who had hurt me did not acknowledge any wrongdoing on their part and were actually very smug about my apology. Yet I could not bring up their offenses! What a killer to my "flesh" and how effective in crushing my pride! Those were the hard ones, but then I went back to my heavenly Father in prayer afterwards, and His mercy poured over me like warm oil. Besides wanting to please God, what helps me not to retaliate now is knowing that He will make me go back to make amends. So making amends also produces self-control, as the fruit of the Spirit. *Radical obedience brings radical blessing!*

Make amends only as the Lord leads, since it would not be prudent or possible in the area of some offenses. In everything, we must be led by the Holy Spirit. The principles are the same for each of us, but principles merely serve as boundaries. Within those boundaries, we must rely on the Holy Spirit for timing and direction in doing His specific will. Confessing offenses that the other party knows nothing about may only cause a deeper wound. On the other hand, the Holy Spirit may lead you to confess infidelity, since true intimacy in marriage is based on honesty and openness. Do not rely on your own human reasoning, but prayerfully seek the Lord's will.

Only after you have made amends, and if their offending behavior continues, should you gently tell others how they have hurt you. Speak the truth in love for the purpose of restoring the relationship. The reason for this is that until you take the plank out of your own eye by making amends, you have *no right* to confront their sin (take the specks out of their eyes).

Some people, however, cannot receive the truth about themselves. Insecure people believe that their worth and value are based on their performance, therefore, they can never be wrong. How do I know this? I spent most of my life as an insecure person, and I always needed to be right. If we are dealing with an insecure person, we are to continue to forgive and wait on God, who makes even our enemies to be at peace with us when we walk in humility and obedience to Him (Proverbs 16:7). However, that peace may have to come at a distance if you are in a relationship with someone who is constantly angry with you, especially because you do not allow him or her to control you. "Do not make friends with a hot-tempered man, do not associate with one easily angered, or you may learn his ways and get yourself ensnared" (Prov. 22:24-25).

I want to make this very clear: Physical abuse is *never* to be tolerated, and that includes threats of violence, which are often used to terrorize and control a woman. If there are children in the home, a mother has an absolute responsibility to remove her children from that environment. It is not only a sin, but a crime as well, and must be referred to civil and church authorities. Where there is no repentance on the part of the abuser, and by that I mean a willingness to enter long-term counseling to deal with underlying issues, there can be no reconciliation.

Offenses that are too serious to overlook (such as those causing serious marital problems, i.e., marital affairs), should be referred to Matthew 18:15-17, which tells us to bring a neutral third party in to mediate. This process may eventually end in church discipline if the offender is unwilling to repent. However, that should be rare if we are applying these principles to our lives. We should not proceed to outside intervention until we ourselves have made amends. I found, in my rocky relationship with my husband, that God required me to demonstrate the love and forgiveness He had been teaching me for about four years before He brought my husband to repentance. But He also gave me the grace to hang on!

Working toward acceptance

When my "self-centered life based on human reasoning" began to unravel, I did not know how to proceed with my life. I contacted a

Christian counselor, who listened to me for a long time over the phone. Her first words to me as I entered her office were, "Donna, your freedom will come through forgiveness and acceptance." How right she was! Just as forgiveness begins with a choice but takes the form of a process, so also does acceptance. How I wish God would just "zap" me and get it over with! But no, that doesn't seem to be His way, at least not with me. I believe He wants us to learn the process so that we can incorporate it into our everyday lives, using the principles again and again, as needed. "He will teach us his ways, so that we may walk in his paths" (Micah 4:2).

What is acceptance? With regard to other people, to "accept" is "to receive willingly."[4] We are to accept others "just as they are" in the same way that Christ accepted us. "Accept one another, then, just as Christ accepted you, in order to bring praise to God" (Rom. 15:7). Easier said than done, wouldn't you say? Apart from God's grace and the power of the Holy Spirit, we can't do it. Do you know that it is *humanly* impossible to live the Christian life? Yet even as we learn to depend on God's strength, we still need to understand what gets in the way of accepting others: our expectations!

To "expect" is "to consider reasonable, due, or necessary."[5] Meekness (humility) is giving all of our expectations to God. That tells me it is my pride that demands from others what I consider to be reasonable, due, or necessary. What we are saying, then, is "I won't accept you unless you are (and do) exactly what I think I deserve, what I think is owed to me, and what I think is necessary for my well-being." *It is our expectations of others that set us up for anger and resentment.*

These demands on our part also express an unhealthy need to control others. We'll be getting into the subject of codependency in Chapter 9, which is the belief that our well-being is dependent on the choices, actions, and emotions of someone else rather than on our own relationship with God. The process of making amends helped to humble me, and it enabled me to see that I had no right to expect others to be and do what I wanted. Rather, I needed to understand that I am not responsible for their choices and behavior—that is between them and God. I had to accept my husband "as is," stop trying to change him, and instead, focus on the changes the Lord wanted to make in my own life. I had to stop "restraining" him—trying to stop him from doing things

I didn't want him to do. In practice, this meant that if my husband didn't come home when I "expected" him to, I would ask the Lord (since He already knew it would happen) what He had planned for me that evening. I began to experience peace and a sense of God's presence as I placed my expectations in Him instead of others. Jesus is love, and "love never fails." Jesus will never "stand you up" for a date!

As I've already mentioned, my relationship with my husband could not have been worse at that point. Let's just say there was a lot of water under that bridge, and in the prior twenty-three years of our marriage, we had hurt each other immensely. Nevertheless, God called me to forgive, make amends, love, accept, and seek reconciliation. Now that was a God-sized assignment! If you recall, mercy is treating someone the opposite of what he deserves, just as Jesus did for us. "But God demonstrates His own love for us in this: While we were still sinners, Christ died for us" (Rom. 5:8). Though it takes two to reconcile, and we don't have any control over how others respond, we can and must take the initiative to move in that direction. We need to obey God, even if others do not. That is all God is requiring of us. "If it is possible, as far as it depends on you, live at peace with everyone" (Rom. 12:18). Leave the outcome in His hands; He will move on your behalf.

Repentance and restoration

The following process of repentance and restoration is not intended to be completed in a brief period of time. This is something you will need to work through with much prayer. And it is work. I can testify to the effectiveness of the following process in bringing healing to my marriage and in restoring other relationships, as well. However, for the purposes of this book, please focus on your relationship with your husband (or ex-husband, if divorced). If neither applies, you can focus on another family relationship.

1. *Face the truth about your life.* Whatever anguish of soul you are experiencing is not someone else's fault. It is a result of your own unresolved anger and prolonged unforgiveness (bitterness). No more blaming. No one can interfere with God's will for your life but you.

2. *Ask God to reveal your sins to you*—sins of which you are unaware, sins about which you've deceived yourself. Ask Him to show you the damage *you* have done, the pain *you* have caused. It will humble and break you in places where you need to be broken: your will, your ego, your pride (your "flesh"). Meditate on God's Word, using the passages we've covered in Chapters 2 and 3:

Matthew 6:14-15	1 Corinthians 13:4-8	Psalm 23
Matthew 18:23-35	Hebrews 12:14-15	Galatians 5:1
Hosea 5:15	Mark 12:30	Ephesians 2:1-7
Ephesians 4:26-27	2 Corinthians 1:3-4	James 1:22-25
Luke 6:32-36	Luke 6:41-42	Proverbs 16:7
1 John 4:20	Galatians 6:7	

3. *Repent.* In the Greek *(metanoia),* repentance means, "a change of mind, as it applies to one who repents of a purpose he has formed or of something he has done." We have to change our minds about our sin: we have to recognize and reject it, and embrace the truth of God's Word. This is where Scripture memorization is so important in replacing sinful thoughts, attitudes, and behavior. Because I felt justified in not loving my husband (wrong!), I found it helpful to memorize First John 4:20, "For anyone who does not love his brother, whom he has seen, cannot love God, whom he has not seen."

4. *Recognize how much mercy you require.* I understood that I could not "undo" the damage I had done to my grown children. Only God could heal them and correct them. It was at that point that God gave me a promise from His Word: "All your sons will be taught by the Lord, and great will be your children's peace" (Isa.54:13). Remember, God's one requirement to experience His mercy is to be willing to extend it to others. When you are willing to do whatever God requires to make things right, cry out to Him for forgiveness and mercy. Then proceed under the leading and power of the Holy Spirit. He will guide and enable you.

5. *Make amends.* Go to your husband and humbly acknowledge all the ways in which you've been wrong: the ways you've shown disrespect (especially in front of the children), the ways you've undermined his God-given leadership in the family, your failure to show love and devotion, the way you've kept a running tab of his offenses (bitterness). Remember, this is not the time to confront your husband about his wrongdoings. God will use your humility to soften your husband's heart toward you.

6. *Make restitution.* Restitution is actually part of making amends. Amends are not complete until we make restitution. This is where you have to "put your money where your mouth is," where you have to back up your words with deeds. Do whatever God requires to repair the damage you've done. Talk to your children, confess your sin of disrespect toward their father, and honor him before them and others. Begin to speak highly of your husband to others, never criticizing him in front of others (be loyal to him). At this point, you may be saying, "Wait a minute, why should I be loyal to him when he is not loyal to me?" As I said before, God brought me to repentance four years before he brought my husband. I'm not saying I did all this perfectly (actually, I went kicking and screaming all the way!), but I wanted my children to be "taught by the Lord" and have great peace in their lives, and the hope of that promise gave me the determination to wait on God.

7. *Release your husband from your expectations.* Instead, look for ways to build him up. Proverbs 14:1 tells us, "The wise woman builds her house, but with her own hands the foolish one tears hers down." When we tear down our husbands, we foolishly tear down our own homes—and our children. God has wired men to need respect and He has wired women to need love (Ephesians 5:33). I believe that God brings us together in marriage to heal each other of our past wounds. Men are healed by the respect of their wives, and women are healed by the love of their husbands. (If you are working on your relationship with your ex-husband, remember that whatever healing occurs there will help bring healing to your children).

Reflection questions

1. If we do not forgive others, God will not *release* us from the burden of our guilt. How does this relate to your life? Could this be the reason you may have been carrying guilt, unable to receive God's forgiveness and let go of the past?
2. Is the Lord convicting you about the damage you have done to your children by disrespecting their father? (He may be your ex-husband, and you've poured out your contempt for him in front of them.) How have you damaged your children in this way?

Will you pray with me?

"Heavenly Father, help us to see our own sinfulness and recognize how much mercy we require on a daily basis. Please bring us to a deep repentance and teach us ways in which we can show mercy to others, especially to our offenders. Help us to release others from our expectations, and trust in Your faithfulness to us. In Jesus' Name we pray, Amen."

Memorization verse

1 John 4:20, "If anyone says, 'I love God,' yet hates his brother, he is a liar. For anyone who does not love his brother, whom he has seen, cannot love God, whom he has not seen."

SMALL GROUP DISCUSSION QUESTIONS

Note to discussion leaders: Before proceeding to the discussion questions, it is helpful to begin by asking the women if there was some point in the assigned chapter that they identified with or that was new to them. If time allows, you may also want to discuss the reflection questions listed at the end of the chapter.

1. Did you begin the "Process of Forgiveness" homework? What did it reveal to you about the ways in which you tend to retaliate against those who offend you?

2. In what ways have you set yourself up for anger and resentment because of your expectations of what your husband (or others) should or should not do? What are some ways that you try to "restrain" or control your husband's (or others') behavior so that you are not negatively affected?

3. Do you find it difficult to go to others and admit you were wrong? How do you feel about going to one who has hurt or offended you and asking him to forgive you for the way you've treated him?

Chapter 4 ❧

Tearing Down a Stronghold of Self-Deception (Part 1)

SCRIPTURE SPEAKS OF the "heart" as the seat of our emotions, thoughts, and motives. When functioning independently of God, the human heart is *deceitful.* "The heart is deceitful above all things and beyond cure. Who can understand it? 'I, the Lord, search the heart and examine the mind, to reward a man according to his conduct, according to what his deeds deserve'" (Jer. 17:9-10).

There are things in our lives over which we have no control, things we didn't cause to happen. However, we bring a great deal of pain on ourselves, and the way to get free is to face the truth and take responsibility for our actions. The apostle Paul tells us in 2 Corinthians 7:9: "yet, now I am happy, not because you were made sorry, but because your sorrow led you to repentance. For you became sorrowful as God intended. . . ."

God does not intend for us to continue in the anguish of soul that comes out of bitterness, but there is a sorrow that God does want us to experience: the sorrow that leads us to repentance and it begins with a change of mind. If you are convinced you are right, will you change your mind? No, why would you? You can see, then, that we have to become willing to face the truth that we have been wrong in order to allow the Holy Spirit to bring us to repentance.

Do you remember the Fonz from the TV program, *Happy Days*? In one episode, the Fonz had to apologize and admit he was wrong. He did his best to get that word out . . . "I was wr— I was wr— I was wr—" He was so proud (and "cool") that he could not admit he was wrong! Let me tell you that it is very "cool" to admit you're wrong. Besides, you'll have to become very comfortable with saying it because, in the repentance and restoration process, you'll find it to be a necessity!

I want to remind you of two truths we focused on in the first chapter. First, all sin is meeting our own needs in our own way, independently of God.[1] The basis of this goes all the way back to the garden, where Satan tempted Eve by convincing her that God did not have her best interests at heart. That's when she began trying to meet her own needs with disastrous results for all of us. The second thing I want to remind you about is that from childhood we begin to live self-centered lives based on human reasoning. We are self-reliant rather than God-dependent. Again, we see that principle working in Eve's decision.

The New American Standard Bible (NASB) uses the term *flesh*, while the New International Version (NIV) uses *sinful nature* to describe the unregenerate nature of the unsaved person. However, the term *flesh* is also commonly used to describe the ego, will, and appetites of believers when we are not functioning under the control of the Holy Spirit. In Galatians 5:16-17 (NASB), Paul tells us, "But I say, walk by the Spirit and you will not carry out the desire of the flesh. For the flesh sets its desire against the Spirit, and the Spirit against the flesh; for these are in opposition to one another, so that you may not do the things that you please."

A battle is raging: Will we surrender to the control of the Holy Spirit or will we succumb to the demands of the flesh? The flesh has a mind of its own (human reasoning). It is cunning and deceptive. Our flesh does not want to surrender control to God, and so we deceive ourselves about our sin. The secular term for this self-deception is *denial*. It is a denial of reality; it is a denial of the truth. We see it at work in addictions where individuals are blinded to the cause of their self-destruction. But we see it at work in *all* our lives. None of us is exempt.

Deceiving ourselves

Don't you just hate it when someone lies to you—looks you straight in the eye and tells you a bold-faced lie? I just hate that! Yet I have learned that I have lied to myself more than anyone else has ever lied to me. The apostle John says it this way, in his first epistle: "If we claim to be without sin, we deceive ourselves and the truth is not in us" (1 John 1:8). Self-deception means that *we deceive ourselves about ourselves.* I've asked the Lord to show me the truth about myself at all cost because I realize that I have practically destroyed my life through self-deception.

Remember that the Lord put on my heart that I had a warped perception of reality. Our perception is the lens through which we see everything. We see God, we see ourselves, and we see the world through our perception. If it's warped, then every judgment we make is wrong, and everything we see is distorted. It's very hard to come to the realization that we have been wrong about virtually everything, and we're going to need a major overhaul. This occurred in my forties and I didn't have enough energy for a major overhaul! God had to do it, but I had to be willing.

Sin warps our perception of reality, and I'm speaking of both our own sins and the sins committed against us. If you think of young children who were abused, perhaps by an authority figure, you can understand why their view of authority is going to be distorted. Their mistreatment affects the way they see themselves and live their lives, since the natural response as they grow older will be to rebel against authority. As is the case for any of us—whether we suffered childhood abuse or not—in order for our perception to be "straightened out," we need to recognize and reject the lies we have believed and embrace the truth. That's what we'll be working on.

In Chapter 1, we sought to line up our view of God with the truth of Who He really is, to know His true nature and character as He has revealed Himself to us through Scripture. We also need to line up our thinking with God's Word as to His view of us. Let's look at Genesis 1:27: "So God created man in his own image, in the image of God he created him; male and female he created them." Based on the Word of God, what gives us our worth and value? We were made in the image of God, which means that our worth and value are intrinsic. In other words, they have been built into us, and have nothing to do with our performance.

For a balanced view, we must also look at Romans 3:23, which tells us, "for all have sinned and fall short of the glory of God." That is also true. We have been made in the image of God, but we were separated from God through sin. Yet we know that our heavenly Father did for us what we could not do for ourselves. The Good News is this: "For God so loved the world that he gave his one and only Son, that whoever believes in him shall not perish but have eternal life" (John 3:16). In God's eyes, we have so much worth and value that even "while we were still sinners, Christ died for us" (Rom. 5:8).

We see then that our worth and value have nothing to do with what we've done or have not done. They have everything to do with God, and what He has done on our behalf. It is in Scripture that we learn of God's view of us. If this is not our view of ourselves, we will spend our entire lives trying to establish our own worth and value through our performance. We see that in perfectionism, we see that in workaholism, we see that in everyone else—but do we see it in ourselves?

If we believe that our worth and value are directly related to our performance, we can never admit we're wrong. We'll defend ourselves at all cost, and we'll deceive ourselves about ourselves. We will only receive the information we want to hear, information that allows us to maintain an idealized view of ourselves. Insecure people cannot face the truth about themselves, and I know that because I spent most of my life as an insecure person.

What does this have to do with forgiveness?

As we become willing to forgive others, we experience the reality of God's love and mercy, which gives us a sense of security. He also infuses us with dignity and self-respect that no one can take from us, and which are not dependent on the approval of others. It's at that point we are able to face the truth about ourselves and admit we are wrong. More importantly, it enables us to see our need for change. The restoration we seek for ourselves and our families begins with recognizing and rejecting the lies we have believed and embracing the truth of God's Word. Our behavior will follow. You can see then that we are not going to get around the issue of forgiveness. We will either deal with the unforgiveness in our hearts, or God will allow us to become so miserable that our lives will come to a screeching halt. The choice is ours.

The victim mentality

We need to look at different types of self-deception, and I've found that a study of the paralytic in John 5:1-9 is very revealing. Verse four is included in the King James Version. However, it is placed as a footnote in the New International Version because it is not contained in all manuscripts. I've included it here because it clarifies the passage:

> Some time later, Jesus went up to Jerusalem for a feast of the Jews. Now there is in Jerusalem near the Sheep Gate a pool, which in Aramaic is called Bethesda and which is surrounded by five covered colonnades. Here a great number of disabled people used to lie—the blind, the lame, the paralyzed [—and they waited for the moving of the waters. From time to time an angel of the Lord would come down and stir up the waters. The first one into the pool after each such disturbance would be cured of whatever disease he had.] One who was there had been an invalid for thirty-eight years. When Jesus saw him lying there and learned that he had been in this condition for a long time, he asked him, "Do you want to get well?" "Sir," the invalid replied, "I have no one to help me into the pool when the water is stirred. While I am trying to get in, someone else goes down ahead of me." Then Jesus said to him, "Get up! Pick up your mat and walk." At once the man was cured; he picked up his mat and walked.
>
> —amplification added

Jesus didn't ask the man *why* he was in that condition, but that's how the paralytic responded. He gave Him excuses; he blamed others. A victim mentality is a type of self-deception. It is the belief that *my unhappiness is someone else's fault.* That's an internal condition of the soul (mind, will, and emotions). The truth is: *No one can interfere with God's will for my life—except me.*

Jesus asked him, "Do you want to get well?" Instead of saying "Yes," he responded by blaming others for his present condition. I think that's a pattern we can all relate to. We're not happy when things don't work out the way we want them to, and we blame others for our unhappiness. I know that I blamed my husband, and no matter what happened, I saw myself as an innocent victim.

"I wouldn't act like a raving maniac if you didn't . . . I wouldn't 'rant and rave' at the kids if you didn't . . ." In my view, nothing appeared to be my fault. I did not take responsibility for my own emotions. Can you relate to that in any way? I would not face the fact that my emotions flowed out of my thought life, and my thoughts were full of bitterness and resentment. And what comes from bitterness and resentment? Anguish of soul!

Do you see how we, as Christians, have an arsenal of excuses for why we aren't living the joy-filled and abundant life? Finally, when I became ready to face the truth about myself, the Lord reminded me that "the fruit of the Spirit is love, joy, peace, patience, kindness, goodness, faithfulness, gentleness and self-control" (Gal. 5:22-23). Those are wonderful things to have, and we cannot blame anyone else if we aren't *experiencing* them. Did you notice that the fruit of the Spirit includes joy? If you belong to Jesus Christ, He dwells within you through the Holy Spirit, and no one else can steal your joy because He is your Joy. Your circumstances won't always be great, but your joy is based on your relationship with the Lord.

Here's another example of a victim mentality: *I am not responsible for my problems.* That's an external condition based on our circumstances. The truth is: *I am the common denominator in all of my problems.*

Everyone has problems in life. That's normal. But if we have continual problems and conflicts with others, then we are the common element in each situation. We need to take a good, honest look at what we're doing to contribute to them. Sometimes we are the problem! That's a hard truth to face, but I found that if everything is someone else's fault, there's not a thing we can do to change a situation. However, if we take responsibility for what is our part, we can change by the grace of God. And if we change, our circumstances will change. That is an awesome revelation that only took me forty-three years to learn!

Remember, "all have sinned and fall short of the glory of God" (Rom. 3:23). No one is innocent. I'm not referring to a specific instance, such as rape or murder or natural disaster, where indeed a person is an innocent victim. I'm looking at our lives overall. As long as we see ourselves as innocent victims, we will not see our need to change and, therefore, our lives will not change. We will continually be trying to change other people, and their behavior and choices, to conform to what we want.

As my former pastor often asked, "How's that working for you?" It has been said that the definition of insanity is to do the same things over and over again and expect the outcome to change. I did the same things repeatedly: blaming someone else for my problems, not taking responsibility for my behavior, yet expecting my life to change. If that describes you, then you need to get the revelation that your life is not going to change.

I realize that this is a very painful process. It is the dismantling of the lives we have built, but it is also the beginning of the sacred journey from the self-centered, self-reliant life to the God-centered, God-dependent life. It does feel as though our lives are falling apart because they are. We struggle to keep that from happening, yet the Lord will tear down the lives we have built on faulty beliefs (strongholds) and will construct a new life for us. That new life is "Christ in you, the hope of glory" (Col. 1:27) and is built on a foundation of truth. "I have been crucified with Christ and I no longer live, but Christ lives in me. . . ." (Gal. 2:20).

The cost of self-pity

Following is an example of self-pity as another costly form of self-deception demonstrated by the paralytic in John 5. We can't know his heart, but I am using his responses as examples of self-deception. Self-pity tells us: *Because of the pain in my life, no one should hold me accountable for my behavior.* Often, we feel sorry for ourselves because of the pain in our lives, which we perceive as being caused by other people. "If only everyone in my life would just straighten up and fly right, my life would be just fine."

We see ourselves as innocent pawns in the chess game of life. Yet crises and chaos conveniently deflect our attention away from our flaws. They enable us to shift blame away from ourselves and see our bad behavior as a natural result of difficult circumstances. Years ago, the Lord impressed upon me that I was paying a very high price for self-pity: it kept me trapped in a pitiful life rather than engaged in the victorious life of freedom that Christ died to give me. Self-pity leads us to believe that if we can make others feel sorry for us, they will excuse our bad behavior. Now think about why we complain about someone. For example, if we can convince others that our husbands are "ogres" (that's what I did), we can make them feel sorry for us. If that's how we justify our behavior, don't you know we'll portray others unfairly in order to present ourselves as innocent? That's what the paralytic did, and that's what I did, but the truth is: *We all have painful circumstances in our lives. That does not justify our sin. We are justified by the blood of Christ alone.*

I knew that God saved me by His grace, through my faith in Christ alone (Ephesians 2:8). That's the basis on which we're saved. However, we have to question our unconscious beliefs (mental strongholds) if we're acting as if we're justified by the pain in our lives. That's not what justifies us. Wrong is wrong no matter what anyone else has done to us or what painful condition we find ourselves in. I hope you embraced that truth in Chapter 3, when we had to make amends for our sinful responses to those who had hurt us. We'll have to ask the Lord to turn His searchlight on our *unconscious beliefs*—those things we haven't faced yet. He will lovingly do that as we seek Him in prayer and through His Word. "Search me, O God, and know my heart; test me and know my anxious thoughts. See if there is any offensive way in me, and lead me in the way everlasting" (Ps. 139:23-24).

Let's look further at the story of the paralytic, as John 5:14 tells us, "Later Jesus found him at the temple and said to him, 'See, you are well again. Stop sinning or something worse may happen to you.'" Jesus didn't give this man pity because he didn't need pity. He needed the truth, and it often takes more love to tell someone the truth than to tell him what he wants to hear. Instead, Jesus confronted the paralytic with his own culpability in his situation. Since the passage tells us that he was *physically* crippled, Jesus must have been speaking of sinning in his thought life and attitudes rather than in his actions.

Self-pity and resentment come from sinful thoughts that, over time, develop into sinful attitudes (mental strongholds). How many of us are emotionally crippled by the self-pity and resentment in our lives? We look longingly at the joyful and blessed lives we see other people enjoying, and seek to blame someone or something else for the fact that we don't have that kind of life. Isn't that what the paralytic did?

We may unknowingly perpetuate our problems in order to receive pity because it "fits" our perception of ourselves as victims. We can react to a situation in such a way that we always end up being a victim. I'm going to use rescuing people as an example, specifically rescuing our older children. Let me remind you that God uses consequences to bring us to repentance and teach us His ways. With that in mind, let's say we have teenagers, and they get into trouble at school. Suppose we take their side and feel sorry for them, and don't make them suffer consequences—we rescue them. Then, because they've had no consequences, there is no deterrent, and their behavior becomes even more rebellious and irresponsible. We continue to bail them out, but who suffers? Not them—we do. We feel sorry for ourselves because of what "they're putting us through," when in reality we have brought it on ourselves.

The deception of pride

For our final study on self-deception, you may be able to relate to what could have been called my motto: *I'm right, and I know what's best.* I realize that not every reader is married, but I'm sure you can still relate. No matter what my husband's idea was, no matter what he wanted to do, I believed that I was right and I would make sure we did what I wanted to do. Then, if it didn't work out, I blamed my husband! Consider this: If you think you're right when you're actually wrong, you'll think someone else is wrong when they're actually right. Then you'll make bad decisions based on bad information, but you'll blame someone else, because you think you're right! Even if I was technically right about a certain decision, I was wrong because I undermined my husband's authority in the home (we'll study more on that in Chapter 10). Proverbs 14:1 tells us, "The wise woman builds her house, but with her own hands the foolish one tears hers down."

In 1990, we had a house fire that gutted our home and destroyed all the contents. All we had left were the clothes on our backs. Fortunately, there were no injuries and we had insurance coverage, so it was no real disaster. However, restoring the house proved to be hard work and required many decisions. Would you believe I would not let my husband make any of them? (I know—you're shocked!) No matter what he said, I knew best and I made sure I got my way. (Does that sound familiar to you?) I knew exactly what I wanted, and I made all the calls to the contractor, often making decisions without consulting my husband. By this time, my husband had learned it simply was not worth making any decisions in our house because if he made a mistake there would be unpleasant consequences. (He lovingly referred to me as the "Tasmanian Devil.")

Larry turned everything over to me and just tried to stay out of the way. When we received the money to replace the contents of the home, I decided what would be spent where, and would you believe that the money ran out before we could replace things like . . . clothes! I didn't realize how much money it would cost to replace all of our clothing and used up most of the money on furniture and appliances. I so mishandled things! Even so, did I admit I was wrong? Did I ask for his forgiveness? Oh, no. "You (Larry) should have helped me make all these decisions. You let all this pressure fall on me!"

At this point, half of the women reading this are thinking, *Well, I'm not like that. I would never act that way.* The other half is thinking, *Yeah, that would be me!* When I rejected my husband's leadership, I was tearing down my house with my own hands. That is what we do when we think we're always right and that we know best. The truth is: *Our need to be right is destroying our relationships and our very lives.*

I call it being "dead right." We bring death to our relationships. We win the battle but lose the war. It is the deceptiveness of pride that convinces us we are right, but it is because of our insecurity, and not knowing that our worth and value have already been established by God, that we need to be right. In every conflict, in every relationship, we virtually lose sight of what the argument is about because we are so insistent on proving that we're right. We'd rather destroy the relationship than let the other person think *he* was right.

Actually, the house fire turned out to be one of many things God allowed in my life to bring me to the point where I could not go on as I had. I've learned that my circumstances did not create the stress in my life, but rather, it was the way I reacted to them. What a fool I had been. I began to see my name written throughout the book of Proverbs: "the fool . . . the fool . . . the fool." I've learned that it doesn't matter what I think because I have been so wrong. The only thing that matters is, "What does God's Word say?"

Therefore, we have a choice to make. Will we continue to deceive ourselves, functioning out of our flawed human reasoning, or embrace the truth of God's Word, which is the mind of Christ? Whose mind do you want to function out of—yours or His?

Reflection questions

1. Ask the Holy Spirit to show you the sins you are blinded to in your own life, and the ways in which you have indulged in the desires of the flesh.
2. Jesus is asking us, "Do you want to get well?" Are you spiritually "stuck" and want to blame others for your unhappiness? What are the areas in which you see yourself doing that, and who are you blaming?
3. Who have you been rescuing? What has it cost you?
4. What relationships have you destroyed because being right seemed more important than your relationship with the other person? If you are divorced, could it have been your previous marriage relationship? How so?

Will you pray with me?

"Gracious heavenly Father, You are so good to me, and that is the truth. Your love for me is so deep and so wide. I pray that You would enable me to face the truth about myself. What is it (in me) that causes me to seek pity from others? How am I deceiving myself through my self-pity? Please forgive me and show me the truth about myself. Shine Your light on the deepest recesses of my soul—my mind, my will, and my emotions. Expose the lies through which the enemy has deceived me since childhood. Enable me to confront them, reject them, and receive Your wonderful Word. In Christ's Name, I pray. Amen."

Memorization verse

Jeremiah 17:9, "The heart is deceitful above all things and beyond cure. Who can understand it?"

SMALL GROUP DISCUSSION QUESTIONS

Note to discussion leaders: Before proceeding to the discussion questions, it is helpful to begin by asking the women if there was some point in the assigned chapter that they identified with or that was new to them. If time allows, you may also want to discuss the reflection questions listed at the end of the chapter.

1. Describe an instance in your life when you deceived yourself about yourself:
    (a) by seeing yourself as an innocent victim, (b) through self-pity, (c) by thinking you were right when you were actually wrong.
2. Can you think of a situation where you rescued someone from the consequences of his or her actions and then felt sorry for yourself as a result?
3. As you think about yourself in these situations, what feelings do they evoke? Are you embarrassed, surprised, or grateful for the revelation?

Chapter 5 ❧

Tearing Down a Stronghold of Self-Deception (Part 2)

IT SHOULD BE evident by now that we all need to ask the Lord to show us the truth about ourselves. Just so you know that I continue to do that, I want to tell you my cell phone story.

One day, just a few years ago (when I should have known better), I allowed myself to have a wrong attitude toward my husband. I remember him standing at the kitchen counter, making a sandwich, and I proceeded to talk to him concerning changes I felt he should make. I was just trying to help him see the error of his ways, of course. It seemed to me that I handled it very well, but that man totally ignored me and kept making his sandwich. Would you believe he paid no attention to me at all?

Well, I thought, *I'll call Julie* (my daughter), *because she listens to me.* She lives in Atlanta, so I picked up my cell phone to make the long distance call and saw that I had a message. I thought it might be from Julie, so I decided to retrieve it before calling her. I have no idea how this happened, but the message I retrieved was a recording of every word I had just said to my husband!

Let me tell you, if you had a similar conversation, you might hear what I heard: a very self-righteous and petty person. Who did I think I was? Horrified and humbled, I realized once again that dealing with my own shortcomings is a full-time job, leaving no time to work on others.

Keep asking the Lord to show you the truth about yourself, and I can assure you that He will find very creative ways to do that!

Self-deception as a stronghold

Review and repetition: that's how I learn. How about you? In Chapter 1, I referred to the following passage, but now I would like to go deeper into its meaning:

> For though we live in the world, we do not wage war as the world does. The weapons we fight with are not the weapons of the world. On the contrary, they have divine power to demolish strongholds. We demolish arguments and every pretension that sets itself up against the knowledge of God, and we take captive every thought to make it obedient to Christ.
> —2 Cor. 10:3-5

We see from these verses that strongholds can only be demolished or torn down by the use of divine weapons. Why? Because they have spiritual roots: they are a fortress of lies built up in our thinking by the enemy of our souls. That's why secular counseling can only modify behavior. It has no power to replace the lies we have believed with the truth of God's Word and thereby transform a human heart.

In the Greek, "arguments" (*logismos*) means "a reckoning, computation; a reasoning: such as is hostile to the Christian faith." Sounds like human reasoning, doesn't it? It's "adding up the facts" as we see them, and coming to a conclusion that is contrary to God's Word.

I can relate to this as I think back to my early years as a Christian. I attended a Bible study led by a godly older woman, and she was teaching on the wife's submission to her husband's position of authority in the home. I thought, *That may work for some women, but it certainly wouldn't work in my marriage.* I added up the facts (as I saw them from my human reasoning) and assigned them a place of higher authority than God's Word. I believed a lie, and that lie distorted my perception of the truth.

In the above passage, the New International Version also uses the word *pretension*, which comes from the word *pretense*, defined as "an unjustifiable claim: one not supported by fact; a false show."[1] Are you getting the picture? A "pretense" is deceptive and explains Satan's methods in building the stronghold. Again, let me make it clear that Satan has no authority over the believer, but if he can entice us to believe lies (as he did Eve in the garden), he can wreak havoc in our lives. We are commanded to tear down these mindsets, not ignore them or justify them. We are to wage war against the lies of the enemy, bringing them as conquered foes into submission to the authority of God's Word.

Deceived by a worldly philosophy

Now, let me give you another example of a stronghold of self-deception. When women have been abused by a male authority figure in their childhood, they will naturally react by rejecting male authority as adults. I know this firsthand, and my heart goes out to these women. However, this mindset is a form of self-deception that the Lord has had to deal with in my own life: *feminism.* I am not referring to a woman's God-given rights, protection, opportunity, or equality. Scripture teaches that we are to defend the rights not only of women, but of all who are hurting or oppressed. "Is not this the kind of fasting I have chosen: to loose the chains of injustice and untie the cords of the yoke, to set the oppressed free and break every yoke?" (Isa. 58:6 NIV)

The modern-day feminist movement, however, promotes women's *desires*, often at the expense of marriage and family. Diane Passno, executive vice president at Focus on the Family, writes in her book, *Feminism: Mystique or Mistake?*: "The secular feminist agenda thrives in a postmodern culture, since the movement is basically selfish or self-centered in nature. It's all about women and what they want, and has nothing to do with what is healthy for all members of the culture."[2]

If we do not reject it, feminism will distort our perception of the truth of God's Word and render us *incapable* of fully surrendering our lives to the will and purposes of God. If we deny this truth, we are deceiving ourselves. Furthermore, if we don't reject feminism as a worldly philosophy that has been built up in our thinking, we will not be able to embrace God's design for marriage. Diane Passno continues in *Feminism: Mystique or Mistake?*:

To understand the Christian worldview regarding male and female roles, one has to stick closely to Scripture. Christian women often become confused because they take the feminist dogma they have been indoctrinated with and try to make Scripture bend to it instead of the other way around.[3]

That's what a stronghold does: it sets up preconceived ideas that filter the truth of God's Word, causing us to distort truth in order to make it line up with our reasoning. We will unknowingly misinterpret the Word of God and believe that we are correct. However, let me state plainly: *Feminism is not about equal rights for women. It is a self-centered, self-serving, self-promoting worldly philosophy that has no place in the church.*

Those with a feminist mindset actually prove my point. If their agenda were truly about promoting equal rights for women, they would ensure the right of every woman to express her views. Yet I have had feminists try to silence my voice because it opposes what they believe. That's not freedom; that's not equal rights. In order to demonstrate the truth about feminism through Scripture, let me take you to Philippians 2:5-8, which tells us:

> Your attitude should be the same as that of Christ Jesus: Who being in very nature God, did not consider equality with God something to be grasped, but made himself nothing, taking the very nature of a servant, being made in human likeness and being found in appearance as a man, he humbled himself and became obedient to death—even death on a cross!

Let's remember that Jesus Christ is God in human form (fully God and fully man), and the second person of the Trinity: Father, Son, and Holy Spirit. Though equal with God the Father, He willingly became subordinate to the Father for the good of "the plan." In this case, it was the plan of salvation. Our salvation! In addition, I want to look at the marriage relationship as described by the apostle Paul in Ephesians 5:22-23: "Wives, submit to your husbands as to the Lord. For the husband is the head of the wife as Christ is the head of the church, his body, of which he is the

Savior." Therefore, in the same way that Christ is the head of the church, the husband is the head of the wife.

The husband fulfills the *role* of Christ in marriage. Feminists oppose role distinctions in marriage because they see the wife's submission to her husband as oppressive. Feminists (and they're not all women) would quickly point to verse 21, which tells us, "Submit to one another out of reverence to Christ," to insist that the husband does not have a position of authority over the wife. However, when we study the relationship between Christ and the church in Ephesians 5:22-33, we see that the mutual submission referred to in verse 21 may be expressed in this way: "The husband is to submit to his wife's need, and the wife is to submit to her husband's lead."[4]

I want to make the point here also that when we get to Chapter 10, we will look at what is true biblical submission. It is not being a "doormat." It is *never* accepting abuse, and it is not suppressing a woman's personality. Wives, equal to their husbands in every way, are called to respect their husbands' God-ordained position of authority in the home, which is for the benefit of the wife, for the protection of the children, and for the preservation of the family. The world cannot understand that concept, but it is for the good of "the plan." In this case, it is God's plan for the family.

When a woman is fully surrendered to the will and purposes of God, there is not a man on earth who can prevent her from fulfilling her destiny in Christ. And it is an awesome destiny!

Sober judgment

We need to move on to another area of self-deception. I'm making what may appear to be a radical shift in direction, as we look at the biblical definition of the term *sober*. We will see, however, that the lack of sobriety is a state of mind having everything to do with the stronghold of self-deception.

Are you sober? You may be thinking that I'm referring to drugs and alcohol, and perhaps you've never been drunk a day in your life. However, how does God define sobriety? (Have you noticed that we need to keep asking how God defines the terms? We cannot allow the secular world to define these terms because its definitions are not based on truth.) Let's look at Romans 12:1-3:

> Therefore, I urge you, brothers, in view of God's mercy, to offer your bodies as a living sacrifice, holy and pleasing to God—this is your spiritual act of worship. Do not conform any longer to the pattern of this world, but be transformed by the renewing of your mind. Then you will be able to test and approve what God's will is—His good, pleasing and perfect will. For by the grace given me I say to every one of you: Do not think of yourself more highly than you ought, but rather think of yourself with sober judgment, in accordance with the measure of faith God has given you.

We see that we are to be transformed by the renewing of our minds. In the Greek (*nous*), the word *mind* means "faculty of perception." Remember that our perception is the lens through which we view everything. What had God spoken to my heart about my "faculty of perception"? He impressed on me that my perception of reality was warped, that my thinking was distorted.

We are also told in the above passage: "Do not think of yourself more highly than you ought, but rather think of yourself with *sober* judgment." This speaks of a realistic perception of ourselves versus self-deception. However, the word *sober* means so much more. The Greek root for sober *(sophron)* means: "of a sound mind, sane, in one's senses; curbing one's desires and impulses, self controlled." These meanings go hand in hand: If we don't curb our desires and impulses, we're not of sound mind, we're not sane—we're not sober.

Self-indulgence is a failure to curb our desires and control our impulses and will therefore warp our perception of reality and impair our judgment, causing us to deceive ourselves. An example of this would be someone who is arrested for DWI ("driving while intoxicated"). Why is he or she charged for this crime? This person has indulged his desire and impulse for alcohol to the extent that his judgment has been impaired, and he is not safe to drive on the road. In addition, he is deceiving himself because he believes he's fine!

Do you remember the story of the prodigal son in Luke 15? He asked his father for his share of the estate and traveled to a far country, where he proceeded to squander his inheritance in a sinful lifestyle. When he had spent all he had, he had to take a repugnant job—feeding pigs. He came to his senses when he saw where his self-indulgence had taken him: he had lost everything and actually hungered for the food the pigs were eating.

Do you see that when we indulge our appetites and impulses, rather than curbing them, we're not sober? We need to look at ourselves for a lack of sobriety that we think only occurs through the use of drugs or alcohol. The fact is that we all have areas where we indulge ourselves at times. In my case, I would have to say that food is my area of weakness, and as I look around, I can see that I'm not alone! Within the church, we need to look at the fact that we are not sober when we indulge our "flesh."

Dying to the flesh

Galatians 5:13 (NASB) tells us, "For you were called to freedom, brethren; only do not turn your freedom into an opportunity for the flesh. . . ." The flesh is the self-life: one's ego, will, and appetites functioning independently of God.[5] That not only refers to one's unrestrained physical appetites. Our egos and wills also have appetites! Flesh patterns are sinful habits formed like the ruts in a country road. Each time we commit willful sin in any area (such as gluttony, gossip, unforgiveness), it's like driving a car in the same ruts, over and over again, forming a track. Soon those ruts become so deep, it would take a tow truck to pull the car out. That's a picture of us when we do not say "no" to our flesh, when we do not curb our impulses and appetites. A battle is raging within us: will we surrender to the control of the Holy Spirit, or will we succumb to the demands of the flesh—running our own lives, doing what we *feel* like doing?

I always used food for the wrong reason. It had been my main source of comfort as a child, and overeating became a habit that I brought into my adult life. For years, I struggled with a craving for food, especially sweets. (Sugar was my "drug of choice.") In my younger days, I could get away with those extra calories. I was more active and could burn them off. As I got older, however, I was less able to do that and began to put on weight. Do you know that if you aren't forced to confront certain issues, you won't? Fortunately, God will allow consequences in order to "get in our faces" about something we need to deal with. Actually, eating too much sugar is not healthy, whether I gain weight or not. Many of us look to fad diets to get the pounds off. However, do you think our weight is the real issue in God's mind? I don't. I think He wants us to deal with the fact that our physical condition is a result of indulging our (sinful) cravings and refusing to curb our impulses and desires. We are not under the control of the Holy Spirit; we are under the control of our appetites. We're not sober!

In Galatians 5:16-17 (NASB), the apostle Paul tells us, "But I say, walk by the Spirit, and you will not carry out the desire of the flesh. For the flesh sets its desires against the Spirit, and the Spirit against the flesh; for these are in opposition to one another, so that you may not do the things that you please." We see that the way to control our impulses and sinful desires is to "walk by the Spirit." What does that mean? It means to live in His power, seeking His influence and control in our lives. It means obedience to His promptings and surrendering our wills to His. "But the fruit of the Spirit is love, joy, peace, patience, kindness, goodness, faithfulness, gentleness, and self-control" (Gal. 5:22-23). The Greek for *self-control* is *egkrateia*: "the virtue of one who masters his desires and passions, esp. his sensual appetites." Self-control is *self*-denial; it is saying "no" to our wills, our impulses and cravings, by the power of the Holy Spirit.

When we are not curbing our impulses and sinful desires, we are functioning in the flesh. We make the mistake, however, of thinking that we can control these impulses and desires in our own strength, by the use of "will power." That may help you lose weight, but it isn't the fruit of the Spirit. It's actually our flesh changing its tactics in such a way that it can maintain control. *Our flesh seeks to hide its function in order to preserve its strength.* Our focus is still on food. The Holy Spirit produces the true fruit of self-control, and the focus is always on God.

Instead of dieting simply to lose weight, we should ask God to crucify *all* of our flesh, as we "put to death the misdeeds of the body" (Rom. 8:13). I want you to recall the analogy I used in Chapter 1, where I described the life we've built as a house. I said that God is not in the remodeling business. He wants to tear down the entire life that we've built. He wants to crucify (put to death) all of our flesh, not just the part we don't like (the overweight part due to overeating. By the way, it's really the sin of gluttony, but doesn't "overeating" sound so much better?).

We can't indulge our flesh in one area (gossip, unforgiveness, jealousy, etc.) and expect to have victory in another area (overeating), because we're not under the control of the Holy Spirit. The good news is that when we repent, face the truth about our sin, and surrender our wills to the Holy Spirit, we begin to "walk in the Spirit." The more we walk under the Holy Spirit's control, the more we are able to say "no" to our flesh, thus breaking its hold on us. It's like throwing gravel into the deep ruts of that country road, finally enabling us to drive out.

Dr. Rockwell Dillaman writes, in *Ministering the Cross of Jesus Christ,* "Dying to the flesh hurts because God is tearing the very fabric of our lives, uprooting practices and attitudes that have been securely in place for years, removing our emotional security blanket."[6] Sound familiar? Somewhat like God tearing down the house that we've built—that self-centered life based on human reasoning? It's painful because God is removing those old coping mechanisms we've been relying on since childhood, as we learned to meet our own needs in our own way. Why would God want to remove our "emotional security blanket"? He wants to break our dependence on anything other than Him. "Praise be to the God and Father of our Lord Jesus Christ, the Father of compassion and the God of all comfort, who comforts us in all our troubles. . . ." (2 Cor. 1:3). God the Father is the source of all comfort, which comes to us through our union with Jesus Christ and by the power of the Holy Spirit. If we're not turning to Him, we're not really being comforted, are we?

If we do not turn to God the Father for the comfort we so desperately need, we will meet our needs any way we can, and the world has a multitude of ways for us to do that. We need to broaden our understanding of sobriety. We often look at others struggling with drug and alcohol addictions and wonder why they don't just "straighten up"; why they don't just stop. However, we need to look within ourselves and see that if we're not turning to the Father for comfort, we're using *something* to medicate our emotional pain in the same way as drug addicts and alcoholics. Knowing that fact should take all the judgment out of our hearts, shouldn't it?

Surrendering control to God

Our self-willed, self-centered flesh does not want to surrender control to God, and so we will deceive ourselves about its operation in our lives. Dr. Rockwell Dillaman writes further in *Ministering the Cross of Jesus Christ:*

> There are substitutes for dying to self! One among them is legalism. Legalism aborts relationship with both God and others by its negative focus. The evil we seek to avoid grows, with concentration, into targets we cannot miss. Rules, instead of limiting our sin, define sin, rivet our attention to it, and lead us to desire it. In legalism, the flesh is in charge, taking the Holy Spirit's place and thus being strengthened.[7]

This can relate to any number of things, but again, I'm thinking here of the sin of gluttony and our own efforts to conquer it by means of rules rather than relationship. Dieting has become an obsession for many of us. It "rivets our attention" on what we are or are not eating, rather than focusing on God and depending on the Holy Spirit's power to produce the fruit of self-control in us. (I'm not speaking here of medically necessary diets, but even those should be submitted to the leading of the Holy Spirit, depending on His power). Dieting can be another way of meeting our own needs in our own way, independently of God, yet it looks so good.

Instead, God calls us to "walk by the Spirit and [we] will not carry out the desire of the flesh" (Gal. 5:16 NASB). Do you see the priority in this verse? While we are studying the flesh in order to be wise concerning its operation in our lives, the only way to stop indulging our flesh is to "walk by the Spirit." What is the pattern we are to follow? Focus our attention on our relationship with God. God has put a sense of hunger (strong desire) in all of us. Don't ask Him to remove it. Ask Him to redirect it to the sweetness of the fruit of the Spirit, which is the very life and virtue of Jesus Christ deposited in us when we were saved, and that craving is to be our passion for God.

That means that while we cannot produce the fruit of the Spirit ourselves, we must be intentional in appropriating God's grace through prayer and obedience. We will know Him (and love Him more) as we walk in the power of the Spirit; we will know Him *by experience.* Isn't that what we want? Isn't that what we all desperately need? "As the deer pants for streams of water, so my soul pants for you, O God. My soul thirsts for God, for the living God. When can I go and meet with God?" (Ps. 42:1-2). Let's not seek to subdue our sense of hunger through diets, but rather surrender it to God. We need to pray for the Lord to redirect our hunger and desires to the One and only Who can truly satisfy, "who satisfies your desires with good things so that your youth is renewed like the eagle's" (Ps. 103:5).

"Lord, please turn my desires toward You. Satisfy my soul as I feed on the fruit of the Spirit, which is Your very life and virtue!"

Dr. Dillaman reminds us that our flesh looks very good while practicing legalism: rules and regulations rather than relationship. However, our flesh is still in control. The issue is always about control: will we keep it for ourselves or surrender it to the Lord? Our flesh will find ways to make us appear to be living surrendered lives, but in reality, we're not. One of the ways we do that is by making concessions, serving the Lord in the ways we want to, rather than obeying Him.

A sober person is a surrendered person. It's not about what we want; it's about what God wants for us. How can we know if we are surrendered to God? True surrender is accepting the people and life circumstances to which God has called us. It is to trust and obey (Proverbs 3:5-6). Then we can know that we will *have* what God wants us to have, we will *do* what God wants us to do, and we will *be* what God wants us to be.

Reflection questions

1. What is your "flesh" pattern? In what area have you repeatedly indulged yourself, creating a habit you can't break? Could it be food, spending, or perhaps striving for recognition? (Your ego has an appetite too!)
2. Are you using ministry at church to escape an unfulfilling marriage or your responsibilities at home?

Will you pray with me?

If you truly long to live a life that is fully surrendered to the will and purposes of God, please join me in the following Prayer of Surrender[8]:

I present myself to God the Father, Son, and Holy Spirit, as a living sacrifice. With the authority of the name of the Lord Jesus Christ, I renounce "the power and persuasion of the evil one, the love of the world and the lust of the flesh." Father, I confess the sin of unbelief; I have believed the lies of the enemy rather than Your Word. I also confess the sin of pride, which caused me to rely on my human reasoning. "[Christ's] divine power has given us everything we need for life and godliness through our knowledge of Him who has called us by His own glory and goodness" (2 Peter 1:3).

I pray that I may listen and believe as I hear or read the Word of God, so that by the power of the Holy Spirit, God's will and purposes will be accomplished in me. Please reveal *my* sin and change me, Lord, so that I would manifest the character of Christ in increasing measure. "If My people would but listen to me, if [they] would walk in My ways, how quickly would I subdue their enemies and turn My hand against their foes" (Ps. 81:13-14). In the name of the Lord Jesus Christ, I claim "that which the blood of Christ has secured." I profess that I am "God's purchased possession on the basis of Christ's shed blood," and I claim the tearing down of strongholds and "all the works of Satan, such as false doctrine, unbelief, atheistic teaching, and bitterness, which the enemy may have built up in my thinking." In Christ's name, and by the power of the Holy Spirit, I pray that my very thoughts would be brought into captivity to the obedience of Christ.

I put on the full armor of God, standing firm and free from fear, with the belt of truth around my waist, the breastplate of righteousness in place, and with my feet fitted with the readiness of the gospel of peace. I take up the shield of faith, the helmet of salvation, and the sword of the Spirit, which is the Word of God (Ephesians 6:10-18).

In the name of the Lord Jesus Christ, I claim every detail of my life for God, so that by the blood of Jesus Christ, the works of the enemy will be destroyed. I thank You and praise You, Father, that You have made these divine weapons available to me, giving me "authority in Christ that is far above all the authority of the rulers, powers, and forces of darkness, so that the enemy must yield." In Jesus' name, Amen!

Memorization verse

Romans 12:2, "Do not conform any longer to the pattern of this world, but be transformed by the renewing of your mind. Then you will be able to test and approve what God's will is—his good, pleasing, and perfect will."

SMALL GROUP DISCUSSION QUESTIONS

Note to discussion leaders: Before proceeding to the discussion questions, it is helpful to begin by asking the women if there was some point in the assigned chapter that they identified with or that was new to them. If time allows, you may also want to discuss the reflection questions listed at the end of the chapter.

1. How have you been influenced by the feminist philosophy? Have you embraced it, and if so, how has it influenced your life choices? What arguments have you raised in your own mind in defense of feminism?
2. Where do you get your "fix"—your instant gratification instead of waiting on God? Facing the truth about ourselves, and what we turn to or engage in to medicate our emotional pain, is the beginning of sobriety.
3. Has God been dealing with you in a certain area, wanting you to relinquish control to Him?

Chapter 6 ❧

A Solid Foundation—
Our Identity in Christ (Part 1)

THE FIRST EIGHT chapters of this book deal with us as individuals; the second part (Chapters 9 through 12) focuses on the family. In these two sections, we follow a pattern of first tearing down our false beliefs and wrong attitudes and then building towers of truth within us, based on the Word of God. In the first five chapters, we looked at the lies we have believed and how they have affected our entire lives—lies about God, ourselves, and the world around us. The remaining three chapters of Part One are intended to build us up and encourage us in the truth of God's Word, first with a study of our identity in Christ and then the person and work of the Holy Spirit.

Coming to understand our identity in Christ radically transforms our lives. A Christian friend, who had struggled with alcoholism for over thirty years, broke free from his addiction when he finally believed what was true of him through his union with Christ. He was able to say about his drunkenness, "That's not who I am." What we believe about ourselves sets the stage for our behavior and for the way we live our lives. That's why I am asking you, "Who do *you* think you are?"[1]

A stronghold of rejection

A young woman, abandoned by her father when she was a small child, developed a stronghold of rejection and came to believe that she was unworthy of love and acceptance. Children are ego-centric, which means they believe the world revolves around them. Therefore, as a child, this young woman believed that her father left because of her. If only she had been a better little girl, if only she had pleased him more, he would not have left. She perceived herself as a "reject": if her own father didn't want her, there must be something very wrong with her. Then, because we always behave consistently with how we perceive ourselves,[2] she soon developed personality traits that alienated others in many ways. When they finally rejected her, they confirmed to her that her perception of herself was indeed correct. All of this happens on a subconscious level, and certainly, the young woman did not want to be rejected but her belief about herself became a self-fulfilling prophecy.

What could be done to help this young woman? Remember that rejection is a stronghold: a strongly held belief or attitude that is contrary to the truth of God's Word, which Satan uses to enslave us to sin. This young woman had trusted in Christ as her Savior, but she allowed herself to be defined by the actions of a selfish father, rather than by the truth of God's Word. "For the Lord will not reject His people; he will never forsake his inheritance" (Ps. 94:14). And, "The Lord your God is with you, he is mighty to save. He will take great delight in you, he will quiet you with his love, he will rejoice over you with singing" (Zeph. 3:17). The same truth that would set this young woman free, is the same truth that sets us all free: our identity in Christ.[3] Who do you really think you are?

What defines you as a person?

Is it the position you have at work or your ministry at church? Is it your abilities (or disabilities)? Does recognition make you feel important; does wearing valuable jewelry make you feel more valuable? When the stock market crashed in 1929, there were reports of men jumping to their deaths from their office buildings—all because they had lost their fortunes. They found their identity in their portfolios, their money, and their possessions.

More importantly, *who* defines you?

Yourself: If you do well, do you become proud; if you fail, do you feel ashamed—as though you have a big "L" on your forehead for "Loser"? Can you trust your evaluation of yourself? Remember that our perception of reality is warped.

The world: Do you allow the world to define who you are, based on its standard of worth and value, which is how you look, what you do, and what you have? You know the answer should be no, but *do you?* If you lost all of your earthly possessions, have you lost your worth and value or your reason for living?

Or God: As believers, our identity, purpose, and destiny were forever established "in Christ" when we were saved. Our worth and value are not based on our performance, but on the finished work of Christ.

Jesus: the Great Equalizer

"Praise the Lord, O my soul. . . . who redeems your life from the pit and crowns you with love and compassion . . ." (Ps. 103:2, 4). Psalm 103 is one of my favorites. Above is the New International Version, but the King James Version states it this way: "He redeems your life from destruction." I don't know about you, but I had been singlehandedly destroying my life and bringing on anguish of soul for years. Of course, I didn't recognize that fact until I reached the breaking point and became willing to face the truth about myself. Up until that time, I had blamed my husband for my unhappiness (how about you?). Have you made a mess of your life? Perhaps you've walked away from your marriage, perhaps even from your own children. Is it possible you've made some terrible choices and are now living with the consequences, with what seems to be no way out? The majority of us can probably relate on some level.

But how does God the Father view us "in Christ"? We read in 2 Corinthians 5:16-17: "So from now on we regard no one from a worldly point of view. Though we once regarded Christ in this way, we do so no longer. Therefore, if anyone is in Christ, he is a new creation; the old has gone, the new has come." Therefore, no matter where we have come from, no matter what we have done, or what has happened to us, our union with Christ gives us a new identity—*the new creation!*

71

I came to a saving faith in Jesus Christ in 1975. With very little knowledge of Scripture, I thought the "new creation" I heard mentioned was a new and improved version of the old me, and that I had received a clean slate. In regard to my sin, I certainly had. If that's all I received, however, it could be said that I messed up that clean slate a long time ago. Instead, the new creation is something God created when He saved us and placed us into Christ, and we can't get in there and mess it up! It has nothing to do with our behavior; it has everything to do with our position in Christ. The new creation is a completely new species, a new spiritual DNA.

Unfortunately, I didn't learn that truth until I had been a Christian for almost twenty years. If I had heard it taught before, it didn't "sink in." The truth is the old "me" died at salvation, and God raised me to newness of life in union with Christ. That's the new creation: Donna in union with Christ. Since the same thing happened to every believer at salvation, we can say that we are all in the same position. That's why I call Jesus the Great Equalizer!

We know that the gospel is "good news," but the good news is also that we are "in Christ" and He has done everything needed for our right standing with the Father. "His divine power has given us everything we need for life and godliness through our knowledge of him who called us by his own glory and goodness" (2 Peter 1:3). Jesus Christ has already accomplished everything needed for life and godliness! What else is there? I've learned that walking by faith means I believe what God's Word states is true, regardless of what I see or feel. We are not to have a "worldly point of view," judging ourselves and others by outward appearances. Though it may not be visible, we are a "new creation"!

Our new identity

From the apostle Paul's letter to the Ephesians, we learn that we have already been blessed in the heavenly realms: "Praise be to the God and Father of our Lord Jesus Christ, who has blessed us in the heavenly realms with every spiritual blessing in Christ" (Eph. 1:3). Because we are in Christ, the believer resides in two realities: "In the heavenly realms" refers to the unseen spiritual realm that we reside in *at the same time* that we live in this physical world.[4] Ephesians 2:6 tells us that we are seated with Christ in the heavenly realms. I can't see myself seated there, so how do I know it's true? Because God's Word tells me it is true. I've made this point before, but it bears repeating. We learn more from Ephesians 1:13-14:

> And you also were included in Christ when you heard the word of truth, the gospel of your salvation. Having believed, you were marked in him with a seal, the promised Holy Spirit, who is a deposit guaranteeing our inheritance until the redemption of those who are God's possession—to the praise of His glory.

It's also important to note that we were placed into Christ and sealed by the Holy Spirit, Who is the guarantee of our full inheritance. If it were up to you and me to make sure we stayed "in Christ," be assured that we would fail. How could anyone, by his own effort, maintain his position in Christ? Impossible! How grateful I am that Christ's work on my behalf is finished. Faith believes what God says is true, regardless of what we see or feel or what our circumstances tell us (Hebrews 11:1). By faith, we are to live out in this physical reality what God says is true of us in the spiritual reality.

Being "in Christ" is both relational and positional

Relational: We have a relationship with God the Father because we are in union with His Son, Jesus Christ (2 Corinthians 5:17).

Positional: We are in right standing with God the Father because we have been credited with the righteousness of His Son (Romans 4:23-25; 2 Corinthians 5:21).

Jesus: the Gift

What we have been studying is an abstract concept: the divine idea of placing us into Christ in order to accomplish all that God has purposed for us.[5] I've mentioned before that I need word pictures or visual aids to help me understand difficult concepts. I'll be using the analogy of a gift box, with Jesus as the Gift.

Have you heard of the "Romans Road" of evangelism, which uses key verses from the book of Romans to encapsulate the gospel message in order to share our faith with others? I want to present to you what I like to call "John's Road" as a word picture for understanding our identity in Christ. I will use key verses from the writings of John the apostle: from the gospel of John, from one of his three epistles, and from the last book of the Bible, Revelation. I hope that in this way you can envision what it means to be "in Christ."

John 3:16 is not new to us: "For God so loved the world that he gave His one and only Son, that whoever believes in him shall not perish but have eternal life." When does a gift become yours? When you receive it! Jesus Christ is the Gift that God the Father has given to the world. As a child, I believed facts *about* Jesus, but I didn't understand that I needed to receive Him for myself, to trust Him as *my* Savior, and surrender to Him as *my* Lord. And I didn't understand that salvation is a gift that I must receive by faith, rather than earn by my performance. I thought God had a giant scale, and on one side were my good deeds and on the other side were my sins. Whichever side had the most weight when I died would determine whether I would go to heaven—or hell. The truth is that whoever does not receive Jesus Christ will not receive eternal life. How do we know that? John tells us in his first epistle: "And this is the testimony: God has given us eternal life, and this life is in his Son. He who has the Son has life; he who does not have the Son of God does not have life" (1 John 5:11-12).

The following verse in the book of Revelation depicts a future scene around the throne of God upon which Jesus Christ is standing as the Lamb of God, surrounded by believers who worship Him. "And they sang a new song: You are worthy to take the scroll and to open its seals, because You were slain and with Your blood you purchased men for God from every tribe and language and people and nation" (Rev. 5:9). As a believer, you are a "purchased possession," paid for by the blood of Jesus Christ. How wonderful to be able to say, "I belong to Jesus Christ."

The final verse is from the gospel of John and takes place just prior to the crucifixion when Jesus is comforting His disciples. "I will not leave you as orphans; I will come to you. Before long, the world will not see me anymore, but you will see me. Because I live, you also will live. On that day, you will realize that I am in my Father, and you are in me, and I am in you" (John 14:18-20). Jesus makes it clear that His disciples (and that includes you and me) are "in Him."

Here is the picture: The Father-heart of God sent His Son as a gift to us so that we could have eternal life, and that life is in His Son. Christ purchased us for God the Father with His own blood. When we received Him, we were placed "into Him," (picture being placed inside the gift box) and brought back to the Father as a gift. Now He is in the Father, we are in Him, and He is in us.

Now, when the Father looks at us, what does He see? He sees Jesus! Since we were purchased for God the Father by the blood of His Son, how precious are we to the Father, regardless of what we have or have not done? God makes a distinction between who we are and what we do. Positional truth means we are in right standing with God the Father because we are in union with Christ and have been credited with His righteousness. Speaking of Abraham in Romans 4:23-24, Paul states it this way: "The words 'it was credited to him' were written not for him alone, but also for us, to whom God will credit righteousness—for us who believe in him who raised Jesus our Lord from the dead."

A word picture that comes to mind here is that of a credit account. In fact, the word *credit* in the Greek is *logizomai,* and it means "to reckon, count, compute, calculate; to pass to one's account." Imagine you have run up a huge debt you cannot pay. In fact, you have. It is your sin debt. At salvation, Christ Himself pays your debt, bringing it to a "zero balance." But wait, there's more! He takes your sin and then places a credit to your account from His own righteousness, a righteousness that more than covers all your needs for all eternity. He does this not in order that we may sin (God forbid). He makes us righteous so that we can live righteously, in agreement with our position in Christ.[6] As Hebrews 10:14 tells us, "by one sacrifice He has made perfect forever those who are being made holy."

The discipline process

Jesus Christ forever established our right standing with God the Father when we placed our faith and trust in Him. I must also make it clear that God cares very much about our character and behavior because

He is ever at work, through the Holy Spirit, to conform us to Christ. Knowing that we are secure in our relationship with God, however, frees us to receive correction from His loving hand. *In this life, in the physical reality, we still sin. But God will deal with our sin as a loving Father.*

We're going to look at Hebrews 12, starting with verses 5-7:

> And you have forgotten that word of encouragement that addresses you as sons: "My son, do not make light of the Lord's discipline, and do not lose heart when he rebukes you, because the Lord disciplines those he loves, and he punishes everyone he accepts as a son." Endure hardship as discipline. God is treating you as sons. For what son is not disciplined by his father?

How do we endure hardship? I go to my heavenly Father for the comfort I need to endure the discipline I need. Remember, He is "the Father of compassion and the God of all comfort" (2 Cor. 1:3). I can do that because I understand that I have been "perfected forever" in His eyes. When we come to understand our new identity and position in Christ, we desire to be like Him. The process is painful, and at times I have gone through it "kicking and screaming" while at the same time asking God to ignore my pleas for deliverance before He had accomplished His purposes. Let's continue with Hebrews 12:10-11: "God disciplines us for our good that we may share in His holiness. No discipline seems pleasant at the time, but painful. Later on, however, it produces a harvest of righteousness and peace for those who have been trained by it."

In the Greek, the word *trained* is *gumnazo,* and it means, "to exercise vigorously." God will give us a workout! Discipline takes many forms, but one of the most common tools I see the Lord using is simply allowing us to suffer the consequences of our own actions. His intent is not punitive (for the sake of punishment only), but rather, it is redemptive: it is to bring us to repentance. God is at work stripping us of worldliness and tearing down that self-centered life based on human reasoning. The discipline process produces holiness, righteousness, and peace. Do you want peace? Forget that anguish of soul. I want peace!

Friends, "Do not be deceived: God cannot be mocked. A man reaps what he sows" (Gal. 6:7). *God uses consequences to bring us to repentance and teach us His ways.* In Chapter 3, I shared with you that God required me to make amends to those I had offended. In some cases, I had to admit to them that I had no right to speak to them the way that I had. It was very humbling, especially because I felt so justified at the time. Can you guess what helped me keep my tongue in check after that? The knowledge that God would make me go back and do it again.

Reflection questions

No matter where we have come from, no matter what we have done, or what has happened to us, our union with Christ gives us a new identity—*the new creation*! How does this statement change the way you might answer the following questions?

1. Have you made such serious mistakes in your life that you've lost hope of overcoming your past?
2. Do you feel inferior to others because of your family background or circumstances as a child?
3. Did something so traumatize you as a child that it has destroyed your sense of worth and value?

Will you pray with me?

We cannot live the abundant life until we have life itself in Jesus Christ. Have you personally received Him, and His death on the cross, as the only payment for your sins? If you believe God's Word, and can pray in full agreement with the following prayer, please do so now. He will receive you, dear one, and you can know that you have eternal life. "I write these things to you who believe in the name of the Son of God so that you may know that you have eternal life" (I John 5:13).

"Lord Jesus, I believe that You are the only begotten Son of God, that You are fully God and fully human. I believe that You led a sinless life and that You died on the cross for the sins of the world—including mine. I believe that God the Father, by the power of the Holy Spirit, raised You from the dead and that You will come again to judge the living and the dead. I ask you to forgive me and save me so that I can be reconciled with my heavenly Father, be filled with the Holy Spirit, and live with You forever. I receive You as the Lord of my life and the Master of my soul. In Your Name, I pray. Amen."

Memorization verse

2 Corinthians 5:17, "Therefore, if anyone is in Christ, he is a new creation; the old has gone, the new has come."

SMALL GROUP DISCUSSION QUESTIONS

Note to discussion leaders: Before proceeding to the discussion questions, it is helpful to begin by asking the women if there was some point in the assigned chapter that they identified with or that was new to them. If time allows, you may also want to discuss the reflection questions listed at the end of the chapter.

1. What gives you your identity? Is it your husband, your career or ministry, your children? We can lose everything, but we cannot lose Christ. Do you see how essential it is to find your identity in Him?
2. If you have received Jesus Christ as your Savior, you have been made perfect and acceptable to the Father through the blood of Christ. How will knowing this truth affect your ability to surrender control of your life to God?
3. Does knowing that you are a "new creation" (in union with Christ) change the way you see yourself? How does God see you? Recall the analogy of being placed into the Gift (Jesus). If your beliefs don't line up with God's Word, will you ask Him to change your perception of yourself?

Chapter 7 ❧

A Solid Foundation—
Our Identity in Christ (Part 2)

WHAT DO YOU do when someone asks to see your identification? Most likely, you pull out your driver's license. As I look at mine, I see it's only valid for four years. Before the expiration date, I need to renew my license and take a new photo. Well, that system works well enough in the physical world in which we live. There is another type of identification, however, that God provided when I was saved, one that never needs renewing: "Donna in union with Christ." Jesus identified Himself with us by taking on human form (Philippians 2:5-8). In this chapter, we'll look at water baptism as a form of identification and a picture of how we came to be that "new creation," as we entered into Christ's death, burial, and resurrection.

We reside in two realities

In order to understand our identity in Christ, we must first realize that "Christians live in two realities at the same time: their physical world and in the heavenlies in Christ."[1] The first is temporary; the second is eternal. "So we fix our eyes not on what is seen, but on what is unseen. For what is seen is temporary, but what is unseen is eternal" (2 Cor. 4:18). It's difficult to comprehend, but we must believe what God says is true of us in the spiritual realm, even though we don't see it. Ephesians 2:6 tells us that we are already seated with Christ in the heavenly realms. Do we see that with our physical eyes? No, because it's a spiritual reality. How, then, can we know that it is true? Because God said it is! *Truth is what God's Word declares to be true.* It doesn't matter what our circumstances are or what our emotions tell us, and certainly not what our human reasoning determines to be true. We have to rise above all of these things to live by faith, based on the truth of God's Word.

Your behavior may not reflect your true identity and position in the heavenly realm. That's what I refer to as the physical reality: the outward behavior that you see. You always behave consistently with how you perceive yourself.[2] Therefore, you must learn and believe what God says is true of you in order for your behavior to conform to your new identity. Though we will never be perfect in this life, we will be changed. We can live holy lives, surrendered to God, rather than controlled by our flesh.

> Now the deeds of the flesh are evident, which are: immorality, impurity, sensuality, idolatry, sorcery, enmities, strife, jealousy, outbursts of anger, disputes, dissensions, factions, envying, drunkenness, carousing, and things like these of which I forewarn you, just as I have forewarned you, that those who practice such things will not inherit the kingdom of God.
>
> —Gal. 5:19-21 NASB

Does this mean we will lose our salvation if we engage in sin? If you examine this list, you may note that we are all guilty of at least one of these behaviors at one time or another, so that none of us would inherit the future and literal kingdom of God. John 3:36 tells us "whoever believes in the Son has eternal life. . . ." If you have received Jesus Christ (the Son) as your Savior, you have eternal life. (You are *already* seated with Him in the heavenly realms.)

What, then, is the Galatians passage referring to? In Romans 14:17, Paul states, "For the kingdom of God is . . . righteousness, peace, and joy in the Holy Spirit." If we engage in sinful behavior, we will not experience our inheritance of righteousness, peace, and joy in the Holy Spirit—in this life. To do these things is to reject Christ's authority in our lives. If we do not submit to Christ's authority and come under all God-ordained authority, we will not walk in the spiritual authority of adult sons in the kingdom of God. We will be as spiritual infants (1 Corinthians 3:1-3). We will not walk in the power of the Holy Spirit to accomplish God's purposes, and we will not fulfill our destiny here on earth. In fact, we will lose eternal rewards (1 Corinthians 3:14-15). Our choices in this life will very likely determine the level of authority we will have as we reign with Christ in eternity (Matthew 25:21).

It most certainly does matter how we live our lives. But we will not lose what we did not earn: eternal life.

The spiritual reality

I want to take you back two thousand years to the time of John the Baptist as he stood in the Jordan River, baptizing those who had come in repentance. Picture him as he placed each individual under the water and lifted him or her up again. "I baptize you with water for repentance. But after me will come one who is more powerful than I, whose sandals I am not fit to carry. He will baptize you with the Holy Spirit and with fire" (Matt. 3:11).

John is speaking here of a spiritual baptism that will be accomplished by the One coming after him, Whom we know to be Jesus Christ. "Baptism" in the Greek is *baptizo* and it means to "immerse, cleanse, and overwhelm," with the idea of a permanent change in the object. That is a picture of what takes place in the spiritual realm as well: we are "immersed, cleansed, and overwhelmed" by the Holy Spirit. It is, in fact, a permanent change that takes place in us through our union with Christ at the moment of salvation. The apostle Paul also speaks of this baptism in 1 Corinthians 12:12-13: "The body is a unit, though it is made up of many parts, and though all its parts are many, they form one body. So it is with Christ. For we were all baptized by one Spirit into one body—whether Jews or Greeks, slave or free—and we were all given one Spirit to drink."

We need to examine Romans 6:1-7 verse by verse to understand how this spiritual baptism occurred and what it accomplished. It is important to note that just prior to this passage, in Romans 5:20, Paul states, "But where sin increased, grace increased all the more." In Romans 6:1-2,

Paul goes on to say, "What shall we say, then? Shall we go on sinning so that grace may increase? By no means! We died to sin; how can we live in it any longer?"

Do you notice that this verse does not tell us that "sin died"? No, in this life, sin is alive and well. It is ever-present.[3] Instead, God tells us "we died to sin." Do you feel like you've died to sin? Do you look like you've died to sin? The fact is that our flesh is not dead to sin; rather, *we* (the new creation) are dead to sin. This is a spiritual reality, something that God has provided through our union with Christ. How did that occur?

Paul goes on to say in verse 3: "Or don't you know that all of us who were baptized into Christ Jesus were baptized into his death?" We know that we were placed into Christ. Why? So that since He died, we died. Not thrilled about being dead? You will be when you realize what God accomplished by enabling us to identify with Christ's death. In verse 4, Paul states. "We were therefore buried with him through baptism into death in order that, just as Christ was raised from the dead through the glory of the Father, we too may live a new life." We have been placed into Christ so that we could—and would—live a new life! Do you see how important it is for us to *know* that? Paul states in verse 3, "Or don't you know. . . ?" Many of us don't know even after years in the faith that this event has already occurred in the spiritual realm.

We have not only entered into Christ's death and burial, but also into His resurrection (verses 5-6): "If we have been united with him like this in his death, we will certainly also be united with him in his resurrection. For we know that our old self was crucified with him so that the body of sin might be done away with, that we should no longer be slaves to sin."

The "old self" Paul speaks of here is the sin nature we all had *before* we came to faith in Christ. We were slaves to sin, and God's wonderful solution to that dilemma was to see to it that the slave died. The old Donna, who was a slave to sin, died—in 1975. The same thing happened to you at the moment of your salvation. Finally, in verse 7, Paul explains what this accomplished: "because anyone who has died has been freed from sin." We see that, while we are not freed from the *presence* of sin, we are freed from the *power* and eternal *penalty* of sin. Sin is present, but we no longer have a relationship with sin. We were the slave and sin was our master; that was our relationship. But when we "died," we lost that relationship with sin.

What difference does that make? Before we came to faith in Christ, we had a sin nature. An unbeliever can do nothing but sin because sin (*hamartia*) means "missing the mark." Human acts of righteousness are "like filthy rags" (Isaiah 64:6). But when we were placed into Christ, we were given a *new nature,* one that is able to participate in the divine nature (2 Peter 1:4) through the power of the Holy Spirit. *As believers, we are still capable of sin, but no longer compelled to sin.*

For years, I tried to "act" like Jesus, but I made it all about behavior rather than an inner transformation. Rather, God wants us to change our core beliefs about ourselves first, and then a change of behavior will naturally follow. We will begin to "live up to" our true identity. If we see ourselves as hopeless sinners, what will we do? Sin! But if we see ourselves in union with Christ, we will be conformed, over time, to his image.[4]

The change in our behavior is not by our efforts but by the power of the Holy Spirit as we believe God's Word and surrender control to Him. This is really an exchanged life: we exchange our sinful life for the life of Christ. We move from operating in the flesh to functioning under the control of the Holy Spirit. "But the fruit of the Spirit is love, joy, peace, patience, kindness, goodness, faithfulness, gentleness, and self-control" (Gal. 5:22-23). This is the character of Jesus Christ, His very life and virtue, being manifested in us. As this truth begins to penetrate our beliefs, we stop striving and acting and it becomes visibly true of us; the character of Christ is developed in us.

This "rest" is difficult for many of us to achieve because it is so contrary to human nature. We are "doers" and believe that if we try hard enough, we can live the Christian life. I've also come to realize that we have to loathe our flesh before we will surrender our will to God. The more we are in God's Word under the leading and teaching of the Holy Spirit, *and the more we are willing to face the truth about ourselves and our sin*, the more we will despise the operation of the flesh in our lives. Instead of resisting surrender to God, we will run to Him, crying out to Him, "Save me from myself; hide me in Your presence! Rule and reign over every particle of my being." Fortunately, the "self" that we are to loathe is not the real "us." Don't forget, we are a new creation in union with Christ, and that is our real identity. Paul continues this theme in 2 Corinthians 5:15-19:

> And he died for all, that those who live should no longer live for themselves but for him who died for them and was raised again. So from now on we regard no one from a worldly point of view. Though we once regarded Christ in this way, we do so no longer. Therefore, if anyone is in Christ he is a new creation; the old has gone, the new has come! All this is from God, who reconciled us to himself through Christ and gave us the ministry of reconciliation: that God was reconciling the world to himself in Christ, not counting men's sins against them. And he has committed to us the message of reconciliation.

As I stated in Chapter 1, the Lord must dismantle our self-centered life. Why? So that we no longer live for ourselves but for Him Who died for us and was raised again. We are also to live that resurrected life. The world judges us based on outward appearance: how we look, what we have, and what we do. But that is not God's viewpoint. What does God the Father see when He looks at us? Do you remember the Gift? Because we have been placed into Christ at the moment of salvation, He sees Jesus! He sees us through our union with Him. He sees us perfect and acceptable to Him through the blood of Christ.

I used to be "Donna" but now I'm "Donna in union with Christ." It's a new species—a new "spiritual DNA." One that never existed before, it has nothing to do with the "old Donna." I believed for a long time that the new creation was just a new-and-improved version of the old me. Believe me, that would never have satisfied God!

What is God's purpose for our new identity? It is to give each of us the ministry of reconciliation. Chapter 12 is entitled, *It's Not About Us.* Having gone through this process to be transformed by the renewing of our minds, we come to our ultimate purpose of taking that message to others in the love of Christ. And what a message it is: Jesus Christ, God in human form, paid for the sins of mankind so that we could be reconciled with the Father!

The physical reality

We saw in the last chapter that Christ has made us righteous so we can live righteously. Then why aren't we living that out? Alan Johnson, in *Everyman's Bible Commentary: Romans,* sheds light on our dilemma:

> But, one may sigh, after all, Paul, aren't we still human? Don't we live in a world full of lust and evil desires? . . . The "evil desires" are the values and lures that lead us away from obedience to Christ. They are the grave clothes that are carried over from the former life to the new. Specifically, they are the habits of sin learned in the old Adamic lifestyle."[5]

In the "old Adamic lifestyle," Johnson is speaking of the first man, Adam, from whom we inherited our sin nature. That lifestyle is that of the natural man functioning independently of God. It is the self-centered life based on human reasoning before coming to faith in Christ. By "grave clothes," Johnson is referring to Lazarus, whom Jesus raised from the dead, after commanding those nearby to remove the large stone covering the entrance of the tomb, as recorded in John 11:41-44:

> So they took away the stone. Then Jesus looked up and said, "Father, I thank you that you have heard me. I knew that you always hear me, but I said this for the benefit of the people standing here, that they may believe that you sent me." When he had said this, Jesus called in a loud voice, "Lazarus, come out!" The dead man came out, his hands and feet wrapped with strips of linen, and a cloth around his face. Jesus said to them, "Take off the grave clothes and let him go."

Do you see what Johnson is pointing out here? He's referring to the strips of cloth wrapped around the hands and feet of Lazarus, done in preparation for his burial. Though raised from the dead, Lazarus could not function until those strips of cloth were taken off, but he could not remove them himself. Someone else had to help him get free from them. I see this as the work of discipleship in the church. When a new believer comes to faith in Christ, he is still wrapped in the "grave clothes," or the "habits of sin," of his past lifestyle. The habitual sins come from strongholds, which we've learned are beliefs and attitudes that are contrary to the Word of God and which Satan uses to enslave us to sin. (Examples: unforgiveness, self-reliance, rebellion.) We need mature believers to come alongside us and help us identify the strongholds that kept us bound in habitual sins.

I've already made the point that insecure people cannot face the truth about themselves. They believe their worth and value are based on their performance. Therefore, they always need to be right. Don't forget: insecurity is a stronghold as well, which produces many different types of habitual sins in our lives. Insecure people walk continually in self-deception because they cannot receive the truth about themselves (speaking as one who knows). Insecurity can also generate a self-righteous attitude because we have to maintain an idealized view of ourselves (like the Pharisees), since our worth and value are based on being seen as "righteous." Again, do you see how absolutely essential it is for us to understand that we have been made perfect and acceptable to God the Father, through our union with Jesus Christ, His Son? And that our worth and value are based on who we are, not what we do? (If you think I repeat myself a lot, it's because I believe we learn through repetition and review.)

Identity vs. behavior

It is very important that we separate who we are (based on what Christ accomplished) from what we do, and our identity in union with Christ from our behavior. When you're reading Scripture, you need to ask yourself if it is speaking of your identity (and eternal destiny) or your behavior and how it will affect your life here. Otherwise, you will misinterpret the intended meaning of God's Word. For example, Jesus said, "But if you do not forgive men their sins, your Father will not forgive your sins" (Matt. 6:15). If you don't understand the difference, you could interpret this verse to mean that you lose your salvation every time you fail to forgive! Instead, it means that in this life you will reap what you sow. God will not release you from the burden of *your* guilt, if you do not release others through forgiveness. But in the spiritual (eternal) reality, we have already been forgiven of all past, present, and future sins, through faith in Christ.

86

But he was pierced for our transgressions, he was crushed for our iniquities; the punishment that brought us peace was upon him, and by his wounds we are healed. We all, like sheep, have gone astray, each of us has turned to his own way; and the Lord has laid on him the iniquity of us all.

—Isa. 53:5-6

On the cross, Christ bore our sin and all of the Father's wrath directed toward that sin. In God's court of law, the Father declared Christ guilty in our place, and Christ paid the penalty through His death. Previously in this chapter, we looked at the passage in Romans 6:1-7. The apostle Paul writes in verse 7: "because anyone who has died has been freed from sin." In the Greek, the word for *freed* here is *dikaioo,* which means, "acquitted." We were acquitted, and Christ was declared guilty in our place. "God made him who had no sin to be sin [a sin offering] for us, so that in him we might become the righteousness of God" (2 Cor. 5:21).

This is the exchanged life: He takes our sin and He gives us His righteousness; He takes our life and gives us His life. When God the Father looks at us, He sees the righteousness of Jesus Christ. It is only as we perceive ourselves according to God's Word as being greatly loved by God and credited with the righteousness of Jesus Christ, that we can live righteously. We have had it completely backwards: we try to live righteously so that God will see us as righteous. Instead, God has made us righteous so that we can live righteously.[6]

I have referred to the fact that we used to have a relationship with sin: sin was our master and we were its slave. But when we were placed into Christ at salvation, we entered into His death, burial, and resurrection. At that point, we (as slaves to sin) died, freeing us from that old relationship, and we now have a new master: the Lord Jesus Christ (Romans 6:1-4). Satan would love for us to believe that we can be the master of our own souls, slaves to no one, but that will never be. Either Jesus will be our Master, or sin will be our master (Romans 6:16). We will either submit to the Lordship of Christ or we will live under the control of our sin-prone flesh.

Do you see how essential it is for us to know the truth of God's Word in order for us not to be deceived by Satan? He cannot make us sin, but he can deceive us into believing that we can keep a rein on sin without surrendering our lives in humble obedience to God. Not true, according to Romans 6:16: "Don't you know that when you offer yourselves to someone to obey him as slaves, you are slaves to the one you obey—whether you are slaves to sin, which leads to death, or to obedience, which leads to righteousness."

Reflection questions

1. In what ways are you still trying to "live down your past" rather than living a new life in Christ?
2. Do you have what the world calls "low self-esteem"? Do you see how it is a focus on the flesh, ever seeking to improve on it? What is God showing you about yourself?
3. Do you see yourself as insecure? How well do you receive constructive criticism? Do you always need to be right?

Will You pray with me?

"Wonderful heavenly Father, we thank You and praise You for the awesome plan of salvation. You have loved us to the extreme. Lord Jesus, we thank You. Your Word tells us that You have already given us everything we need for life and godliness through our knowledge of You. You left no stone unturned; You left nothing undone. Of ourselves, we can do nothing, and in our flesh dwells no good thing. We pray that we would have no will of our own, but Your will only. Break our will, Lord, as only You can. It is in Christ's name that we pray. Amen."

Memorization verse

2 Corinthians 5:21, "God made him who had no sin to be sin for us, so that in him we might become the righteousness of God."

SMALL GROUP DISCUSSION QUESTIONS

Note to discussion leaders: Before proceeding to the discussion questions, it is helpful to begin by asking the women if there was some point in the assigned chapter that they identified with or that was new to them. If time allows, you may also want to discuss the reflection questions listed at the end of the chapter.

1. When you came to faith in Christ, you were placed into Him and credited with His righteousness. Therefore, when the Father looks at you, He sees Jesus! What difference can knowing this make in your sense of purpose, in your security, in your faith?
2. Insecure people cannot face the truth about themselves because they believe their worth and value are based on their performance. What is God showing you about yourself through this lesson? How can knowing that the Father fully accepts us make us secure enough to hear the truth about ourselves?
3. Think about the habitual sins you brought over from your old (unsaved) life (i.e., root of bitterness, victim mentality). How are they affecting your life today? Do you see that we need others to help us see things about ourselves that we are not aware of, so that we can get free of them?

Chapter 8 ❧

The Person and Work of the Holy Spirit

BY NOW, I think we'd agree that we do not want to carry out the desire of the flesh, and so it is essential that we know how to walk by the Spirit. Therefore, we need to know Who the Holy Spirit is and what He has come to do. I attended a Catholic parochial school as a child, and I can remember studying a catechism that taught us "to know God is to love Him." How true that is! Therefore, if we're really going to know God as He has revealed Himself to us, we must know Him as Father, Son, and Holy Spirit. We've looked at our relationship with God the Father and with our Lord Jesus Christ, the Son of God. Now we want to focus our attention on the third person of the Trinity, the Holy Spirit.

Previously, I referenced Matthew 3:11. I noted that the passage tells us that John the Baptist had been baptizing in the Jordan River. At that time, he spoke of One Who would come after him; One who would "baptize you with the Holy Spirit and with fire." Now let's continue in the chapter to Matthew 3:16-17:

> As soon as Jesus was baptized, he went up out of the water. At that moment heaven was opened, and he saw the Spirit of God descending like a dove and lighting on him. And a voice from heaven said, "This is my Son, whom I love, with him I am well pleased."

Whom do we see in this passage of Scripture? We see Jesus, the Son of God; we see the Father speaking of His beloved Son; and we see the Holy Spirit described as "like a dove" descending on Jesus. Then in Matthew 28:19, in the passage called the Great Commission, which takes place after the crucifixion and resurrection of Christ, Jesus refers to the Holy Spirit: "Therefore, go and make disciples of all nations, baptizing them in the name of the Father and of the Son and of the Holy Spirit. . . ."

Seeing God as One, yet revealed in three persons, is a very difficult concept to grasp and every analogy is going to fall short. We must simply take God at His Word by faith. The Holy Spirit is described as the third person of the Trinity (triune God), not at all because He is less in stature. The Father, Son, and Holy Spirit are one in essence, character, and perfection. Any deviation would be less than perfection and, therefore, not God. When we say, "God is love," that statement is equally true of God the Father, God the Son, and God the Holy Spirit.

Some individuals have the misconception that the Holy Spirit is simply a force or a power. That is not true! Over and over again, the Lord Jesus speaks of the Holy Spirit as a person, not as a force or power. In John 14:15-17, Christ seeks to comfort His disciples by speaking to them of the promised Holy Spirit:

> If you love me, you will obey what I command. And I will ask the Father, and he will give you another Counselor to be with you forever—the Spirit of truth. The world cannot accept *him,* because it neither sees *him* nor knows *him.* But you know *him,* for *he* lives with you and will be in you.
>
> —emphasis mine

God the Father sent the Holy Spirit to us as a helper and a counselor. The Greek word for *counselor* is *parakletos,* which means "one summoned, called to one's side, especially called to one's aid." The word *counselor* may have a different meaning from what you had supposed, as it also refers to "one who pleads another's cause before a judge; counsel for the defense, legal assistant, an advocate," and "in the widest sense, a helper, aide, assistant."

How can we fathom the humility of the Holy Spirit, God coming to indwell us, making Himself completely available to us, to be our aide and helper? If only we modeled our lives after Him as servants, if only we humbled ourselves and sought what is in the best interest of others as He does, we would see tremendous spiritual growth in our lives. We can never accomplish that in our own strength and power, but the Holy Spirit has come to enable us to do exactly that.

The apostle John records Jesus' words describing the Holy Spirit as our Teacher, sent by the Father: "All this I have spoken while still with you. But the Counselor, the Holy Spirit, whom the Father will send in my name, will teach you all things and will remind you of everything I have said to you. Do not let your hearts be troubled and do not be afraid" (John 14:25-27). *The Holy Spirit is our dearest friend, our closest ally. He is always for us and never against us!* Why should we fear when we have been given the Spirit of the living God to dwell within us, teach us, plead our cause, comfort us, and aid us in every way in order that we would become like Jesus?

If all of this is true, why do we see so little spiritual power in our lives? Luke writes in the book of Acts of the power of the Holy Spirit. Here, Jesus is speaking immediately before His ascension into heaven: "But you will receive power when the Holy Spirit comes on you; and you will be my witnesses. . . ." (Acts 1:8). The Greek word for *receive* here is *lambano,* which means "to lay hold of in order to use that which is offered." We will not receive the power of the Holy Spirit unless we are willing to be witnesses. Christ's love for lost souls compels us to tell others how they can receive eternal life through faith in God's only begotten Son. The Holy Spirit, given as a gift, indwells us. Let's *receive Him, welcome Him, and rely upon Him.* Let's be willing to do what He desires, and the power of God will come on our lives.

What has the Holy Spirit come to do?

There is so much to study about the work of the Holy Spirit that one chapter cannot possibly cover it. What I felt led to do, however, was to present the "big picture" of what the Holy Spirit came to do. Reverend David Wilkerson, founder of Teen Challenge, wrote the following about the work of the Holy Spirit in *Hungry for More of Jesus:*

> The work, ministry and mission of the Holy Spirit is . . . to wean us from this world . . . to create a longing in us for Jesus' soon

appearance . . . to convict us of everything that would blemish us . . . to turn our eyes away from everything but Jesus . . . to adorn us with the ornaments of a passionate desire to be with Him as His Bride.[1]

The work of the Holy Spirit, then, is to prepare us (the church) as a bride for the Bridegroom, our Lord Jesus Christ. In God's eyes, there are no denominational barriers. The church includes everyone who has trusted Christ as their Savior since the birth of the church at Pentecost, when the Holy Spirit came upon the disciples of Christ (Acts chapter 2).

In this chapter, we will see a beautiful love story unfold before us. It speaks, obviously, of a spiritual relationship. As our Bridegroom, Jesus is our Provider, Protector, and Lover of our souls. As the bride, we receive His provision and protection, and we respond to His love. Jesus is the initiator and we are the responders.

In order to follow this love story, we will need to understand the pattern of the Old Testament wedding tradition. In that culture, the father of the family had the main house, and as sons married, they added onto the main house, sharing a courtyard. The bride prepared herself, not knowing exactly when her bridegroom would arrive to take her to his father's house. In the meantime, the bridegroom prepared a home for his bride, then would go to her and take her to the wedding ceremony and feast. With this in mind, let's read the comforting promise of Jesus in John 14:1-4:

> Do not let your hearts be troubled. Trust in God; trust also in me. In my Father's house are many rooms; if it were not so, I would have told you. I am going there to prepare a place for you. And if I go and prepare a place for you, I will come back and take you to be with me that you also may be where I am. You know the way to the place where I am going.

You can see that Jesus is speaking of the Old Testament wedding tradition, as described previously. At this moment, He is preparing a place for us, and when the Father determines the time is right, He will return for us corporately as His bride, to take us to His Father's house. This is a different occurrence from when an individual believer dies.

At the moment of our deaths, our souls go immediately into God's presence (2 Corinthians 5:8). Here, I am speaking of all believers corporately as the bride of Christ, at the event commonly referred to as the rapture, from the Latin word meaning "caught up." I want to create a picture for you as to how this will all take place. So let's look now at First Thessalonians 4:16-18:

> For the Lord himself will come down from heaven, with a loud command, with the voice of the archangel and with the trumpet call of God, and the dead in Christ will rise first. After that, we who are still alive and are left will be caught up together with them in the clouds to meet the Lord in the air. And so we will be with the Lord forever. Therefore, encourage each other with these words.

The "dead in Christ" (believers who have already died) will not be forgotten. Their souls are present in heaven, will return with the Lord (1 Thessalonians 4:14), and be re-united with their resurrected bodies (1 Corinthians 15:51-55). Those believers who are still alive at the time of the rapture will also be caught up with the Lord *in the air*. Within Christianity, there are differing views as to the timing of the rapture in connection with end-time events. Though I respect the views of other Christians who find scriptural evidence supporting another view, I believe Scripture teaches that the church will be "caught up"—taken out of harm's way—prior to the final seven years of judgment destined to fall upon a Christ-rejecting world. This is a period known as the Tribulation (Daniel 9:24-27; 2 Thessalonians 2:1-7; Matthew chapter 24; Revelation chapters 6-18). In fact, Scripture reveals that the church will return *with Christ* to establish His thousand-year reign of peace on earth (Revelation chapters 19-20). C. I. Scofield states it this way:

> The Marriage Supper of the Lamb is the consummation of the marriage of Christ and the Church as His Bride. The figure is according to the oriental pattern of marriage covering three stages: (1) betrothal, legally binding when the individual members of the body of Christ [the church] are saved; (2) the coming of the Bridegroom [Christ] for his Bride at the rapture of the Church; and (3) the marriage supper

of the Lamb [Jesus] occurring in connection with the second coming
of Christ to establish His millennial kingdom."[2]

—amplification added

The rapture is said to be imminent, which means that it can
occur at any time. So we, as the bride, don't know exactly when Jesus
is coming for the church. Therefore, we're always to be in a state of
expectancy and readiness, anticipating this wonderful event. Jesus said
in Revelation 22:7, "Behold, I am coming soon!" The word *soon* in the
Greek is *tachu,* which means "speedily, without delay." Granted, God's
idea of soon and ours may differ, but John Walvoord explains it this
way in his commentary, *The Revelation of Jesus Christ:* "The thought
seems to be that when the action comes, it will be sudden. Also it is to
be regarded as impending as if it is meant to be fulfilled at any time. In
either case, it constitutes a message of warning that those who believe
should be alert."[3]

Then Christ will take us to Himself, as a bride beautifully clothed for
her wedding, as we see described in Revelation 19:6-8. This scene takes
place in the heavens, prior to Christ's return to earth with His bride.
At this point, multitudes of the saints of God break out in thunderous
praise:

> Then I heard what sounded like a great multitude, like the roar of
> rushing waters and like loud peals of thunder, shouting: "Hallelujah! For
> our Lord God Almighty reigns. Let us rejoice and be glad and give him
> glory! For the wedding of the Lamb has come, and his bride has made
> herself ready. Fine linen, bright and clean, was given her to wear."
> (Fine linen stands for the righteous acts of the saints.)

Please note that "fine linen was given her to wear," and that "fine
linen stands for the righteous acts of the saints." This is not referring to
good deeds that we decided to do on our own. Christ's righteousness was
credited to our account so that we could live righteous and holy lives in
the power of the Holy Spirit. Ephesians 2:10 tells us, "For we are God's
workmanship, created in Christ Jesus to do good works, which God
prepared in advance for us to do." These are certainly not our own good
deeds, but rather, they are God's works that He prepares "in advance for

us to do." All we can do is receive them and then do them in the power of the Holy Spirit, so that they are God's work from beginning to end and He gets the glory. These righteous acts in some way form the very fabric of the bridal gown.

I pray to the Lord Almighty that I may convey to you a sense of urgency. We see the world on its path to self-destruction, moving toward the fateful days of the Great Tribulation. This truth should cause us to turn from our self-centered lives to be purified and ready for the Bridegroom's return. I believe that the Lord will use the events that we see unfolding in the world around us to purify us. He will show us that our fascination with the materialism of our day is but a cheap amusement compared to our high calling in Christ Jesus. And He will show us our greatest need and His greatest gift: the capacity to love, first Him, and in turn, others (Matthew 22:37-39).

The Holy Spirit is going to prepare the church as a bride for the appearance of her Bridegroom, Jesus Christ. I want to examine three things that, out of the many things the Holy Spirit does in our lives, relate to the preparation of the bride. First, He is going to purify us from the love of self and the love of the world. Second, He is going teach us to remain in intimate fellowship with Christ through obedience. And third, He is going to ensure that we are rooted and established in love.

The Holy Spirit will purify us from the love of self and the love of the world. In Chapter 1, I stressed the work of the Holy Spirit in tearing down the "house" that we've built—the self-centered life based on human reasoning. He will cause us to reject that life as a condemned building, a worthless shack. Then He will strip us of worldly desires. The apostle John tells us that we are not to be seduced by the world:

Do not love the world or anything in the world. If anyone loves the world, the love of the Father is not in him. For everything in the world—the cravings of sinful man, the lust of his eyes and the boasting of what he has and does—comes not from the Father but from the world. The world and its desires pass away, but the man who does the will of God lives forever.

—1 John 2:15-17

Many in the church today, here in America and in places abroad, have turned their affections away from the Lord and are in love with the world. Instead of transforming our culture, we have adapted to our culture. Instead of being holy and set apart, we have been assimilated into our culture. Often, we don't look unlike the world. Our divorce rate is the same, our children are broken, and addictions are rampant. And so, I would say that something must happen within the body of Christ, both individually and corporately, in order for us to become that glorious bride, because the church today is in disarray. Only a deep repentance can reverse that condition, and I have full confidence that the Holy Spirit will be able to bring that about.

The Holy Spirit is preparing and purifying us as a bride for the Bridegroom. He is going to make us holy, not only in our position but in our practice, a holy, set-apart people who love the Lord Jesus Christ with all of our hearts, no longer in love with the world. Jesus is not coming for an unfaithful bride; He is not coming for a disinterested bride. He is coming for a glorious bride, holy and without blemish (Ephesians 5:27). We must understand that the Holy Spirit is totally committed to presenting us as a glorious bride, and He will do whatever is required to get us there.

I would like to caution you that we can do this the easy way, or we can do this the hard way. We can cooperate with the work of the Holy Spirit in our lives, as we're seeking to do through this repentance and restoration process, or He can purify us with "fire," a painful burning away of the works of the flesh and our love for the world. He will do so in love, but it is something that must be done. And so, we must be a people who live a lifestyle of repentance: a change of mind resulting in a change of behavior. When the Holy Spirit reveals to us that there is an area of our lives—whether it is our thoughts, our attitudes, or our actions—that needs to change "in order that we may walk in a manner worthy of the Lord" (Col. 1:10 NASB), we must surrender our wills to the Holy Spirit.

In John 15, Jesus tells us, "I am the vine; you are the branches" (verse 5). He tells us that we must remain (or "abide" in the King James Version) in Him. We do this through our union with Him, as a branch receives life from the vine. The Greek word used for *remain* is *meno*, and means "in reference to time, to continue to be, not to perish, to last, endure; in reference to state or condition, to remain as one." But in verse 9, He tells us to remain (abide) in His love, which speaks of our fellowship with Him. This intimate relationship with Jesus is conditional and is based on the obedient response of the believer. "If you obey my commands, you will remain in my love (verse 10). Let me make it clear that all believers are in union with Christ—period. What I am speaking of, and what this verse states, is that our *intimate relationship* with Christ is dependent upon our obedience.

In fact, Jesus makes it clear that He is asking for one thing specifically: "Love each other as I have loved you" (verse 12). Jesus tells us that we cannot remain in intimate fellowship with Him unless we love others as He has loved us. Hmmm . . . this has a familiar ring to it, doesn't it? In fact, it agrees with and reinforces the truth we learned in Chapter 3: "For anyone who does not love his brother, whom he has seen, cannot love God, whom he has not seen" (1 John 4:20b). We demonstrate our love for God by loving others. That is what the Holy Spirit is working into our lives: the capacity to love, the willingness to love, the fullness of God's love. Paul's prayer for the Ephesians is my prayer for all of us:

> I pray that out of his glorious riches he may strengthen you with power through his Spirit in your inner being, so that Christ may dwell in your hearts through faith. And I pray that you, being rooted and established in love, may have power, together with all the saints, to grasp how wide and long and high and deep is the love of Christ, and to know this love that surpasses knowledge—that you may be filled to the measure of all the fullness of God.
>
> —Eph. 3:16-19

If we don't know His amazing love *by experience*, we will look for love in all the wrong places, and the world has a multitude of ways for us to do that. We will live self-centered lives, based on human reasoning. In order to be "filled to the measure of all the fullness of God," we must obey His command: "Love each other as I have loved you," and we do this as an act of faith, through the power of the Holy Spirit (Galatians 5:6b, 2:20).

The Holy Spirit will cause us to be rooted and established in love. How will this be accomplished? I believe this will happen as the body of

Christ comes together in unity. I'm not speaking of compromise on the essentials of Who Jesus Christ is and what He came to do, but rather respecting other believers who share our biblical faith and rejoicing in the fact that we are one in Christ. "How good and pleasant it is when brothers live together in unity! It is like precious oil poured on the head, running down on Aaron's beard, down upon the collar of his robes" (Ps. 133:1-2). The reference to the oil running down on Aaron's beard comes from Exodus 29:7, when God told Moses to consecrate Aaron as a priest. To be consecrated is to be set apart for God's purposes. If we are to serve God's purposes, we will have to come together in unity. We will have to unite on the common ground of our identity in Christ. Alan Johnson puts it this way in his commentary on Romans:

> Individual Christians must not then think of themselves as the whole Church but as petals to the flower. In realizing this truth I must constantly affirm two things: (1) I, or my group, do not have all the truth or all the gifts, and (2) the other person or group may have truth and gifts I do not have. So to be whole I must have fellowship with all true Christians worldwide (and in history).[4]

Unity is an essential doctrine of the Christian faith—not essential for salvation—but essential for the church to mature into the glorious bride.
The apostle Paul, in writing to the church at Ephesus, used the analogy of the head and the body to describe the relationship between Christ and the church and also for the husband and wife. Then, in his letter to the church at Corinth, he used the analogy of a body to describe the function of the church, with Christ as its head: "The body is a unit, though it is made up of many parts; and though all its parts are many, they form one body. So it is with Christ. For we were *all baptized by one Spirit into one body*—whether Jews or Greeks, slave or free—and we were all given one Spirit to drink" [emphasis mine] (1 Cor. 12:12-13).

Do you recall that "baptize" in the Greek is *baptizo,* which means to "immerse, cleanse, and overwhelm"? In verse 13, it is clear that Paul is speaking of a spiritual baptism ("baptized by one Spirit"). There is much controversy in the church concerning the term "baptism of the Holy Spirit." Some believe it occurred at salvation, while others believe it to be a "second blessing." To begin with, we must respect other believers who

100

hold differing views and focus on what we have in common: we were each placed into Christ and credited with His righteousness. I recall standing in my kitchen one day, complaining to the Lord about my husband (again!), when He showed me a picture of Larry (who received Christ as his Savior at the age of eighteen) standing before His throne, wearing a white robe of righteousness (Isaiah 61:10). The Lord spoke to my heart, "Don't touch that." I realized that if I were not willing to see my husband as a believer standing before Him in the righteousness of Christ, I would not be able to view myself that way either and I desperately needed to do that. That is how we are to view all fellow believers.

We see from the passage above that the Holy Spirit baptized us into the body of Christ at the moment of salvation. However, we should long for that spiritual reality to be manifested in our lives through the fruit (Galatians 5:22-23), the gifts (Ephesians 4; 1 Corinthians 12; Romans 12), and the power (Acts 1:6-8) of the Holy Spirit. It is only as we determine to submit to the Holy Spirit in the process of conforming us to Christ, visibly seen as the fruit of the Spirit, that we can rightly function in the gifts and power of the Holy Spirit.

We can look to the life of Moses as an example of the need for the character of Christ to be formed in us. Pharaoh's daughter had found Moses, a Hebrew child, and raised him as her own. When he was grown but still living in Pharaoh's household, he sought to rescue his fellow Israelites by taking matters into his own hands (Exodus 2:12). God planned to use Moses to deliver the Israelites, but first He had to develop Moses' character. God put Moses on the back side of the desert to tend sheep for forty years until it could be said that Moses was the meekest man who ever lived (Numbers 12:3 KJV). Meekness has been described as "strength under God's control." We all know the power and authority that Moses displayed in his life afterwards.

Keep on being filled

We have learned from God's Word that at the moment of our salvation we were given the Holy Spirit as a gift (John 14:26). We also learned that we were sealed in the Holy Spirit (Ephesians 1:13), empowered by the Holy Spirit (Acts 1:8), and baptized by the Holy Spirit into the body of Christ. "For we were all baptized by one Spirit into one body . . . and we were all given one Spirit to drink" (1 Cor. 12:13). I want you to keep this analogy of drinking of the Spirit in mind as you read Ephesians 5:15-18: "Be very careful, then, how you live—not as unwise but as wise, making the most of every opportunity because the days are evil. Therefore do not be foolish, but understand what the Lord's will is. Do not get drunk on wine, which leads to debauchery. Instead, be filled with the Spirit."

The picture here is that we are to drink deeply of the Spirit and keep on drinking. We know that, typically, it takes more than one drink of wine to get drunk. Even so, we are to continue to drink of the Spirit until we are "under the influence" and control of the Holy Spirit. Some of us tasted of the Holy Spirit when we were saved, but have not had a drink since! It may be simply because some have not known how to be filled with the Holy Spirit. Yet God has made it so simple. Jesus said, regarding anything that is according to the Father's will: "Ask and it will be given to you" (Luke 11:9). We need to ask continually to be filled with the Holy Spirit so that we can function under His influence and control.

Now we want to look at what stops us from being filled with (under the influence and control of) the Holy Spirit. When we sin, we reject the Holy Spirit's leading and, instead, "carry out the desire of the flesh" (Gal. 5:16 NASB). Ephesians 4:29-31 makes it clear that sin grieves the Holy Spirit.

> Do not let any unwholesome talk come out of your mouths, but only what is helpful for building others up according to their needs, that it may benefit those who listen. And do not grieve the Holy Spirit of God, with whom you were sealed for the day of redemption. Get rid of all bitterness, rage and anger, brawling and slander, along with every form of malice.

Please note the word *slander*. This is the Greek word *blasphemia,* and it means "slander, detraction, speech injurious to another's good name." If we understand that all believers are part of the body of Christ, we can see why it would grieve the Holy Spirit when we do harm to another's reputation. We are attacking the body of Christ and destroying the unity essential to our growth. God also tells us (we can't get away

102

from this) to get rid of bitterness, from which these other sins emerge. Again, recall what we learned in our earlier study: until we deal with the unforgiveness in our hearts, we are going nowhere in the Christian life. There will be no spiritual growth because we won't be filled with the Holy Spirit, and growth only occurs while we are under the influence and control of the Holy Spirit.

We see from the above passage that we grieve the Holy Spirit through sin, especially sins stemming from our failure to love others. However, we also find that we can put out the Holy Spirit's "fire," His purifying influence, through unbelief. "Do not put out the Spirit's fire; do not treat prophecies with contempt. Test everything. Hold on to the good. Avoid every kind of evil" (1 Thess. 5:19-22). Prophecy (*propheteia*) is a gift of the Holy Spirit (1 Corinthians 12:10), and is "a discourse emanating from divine inspiration and declaring the purposes of God, whether by reproving and admonishing the wicked, or comforting the afflicted. . . ." We're not to put out the Holy Spirit's purifying influence by treating prophecy with contempt. Instead, we're to test and make sure that what is said lines up with the Word of God, and "hold onto what is good."

We should be very willing to allow the Holy Spirit to speak to us through other believers, as we test everything by the Word of God. When Klaus rebuked me concerning my failure to love my husband, he did so because the Holy Spirit moved him to speak prophetically into my life. I thank God for that! Yet I wasn't willing to hear until I became desperate. How many of us have refused to receive a word of correction from another believer, or even an unbeliever for that matter, since God can use anyone? I seem to recall a story in the Old Testament where God spoke through a donkey! (See Numbers 22:28-30.)

For the soon-coming wedding supper of the Lamb

In December of 1996, I was kneeling by my bed during a time of intercessory prayer, completely awake, when I saw before me a vivid blue sky with white billowy clouds. I was seeing it as though I was at eye-level with the clouds. I could only see as far to the left or right as my eyes could move. I could not move my head. Before my eyes, I saw two angels pulling a billowy train of beautiful white fabric from a scroll in the bottom left corner of my field of vision.

The strong forearms of a man held the scroll on each end. The man was outside my field of vision. Each angel held a corner of the fabric, pulling it from the bottom left corner to the upper right corner of my field of vision, up into the heavens. Immediately, I thought what beautiful fabric it was . . . fabric ideal for making a wedding gown. An inaudible voice answered my thought, "This fabric is for the bridal gown of the bride of Christ, which is being prepared even now for the soon-coming wedding supper of the Lamb."

As I marveled at what the voice had just said, I saw a figure in a black hooded robe move from the upper left side of the vision, carrying an old-fashioned coal bucket filled with black coal dust. His face and hands were not visible. He moved toward the center and hurled the contents of the bucket at the stream of white fabric. I cried out, "No!" but was powerless to stop him. From the right side of my vision came a powerful wind, blowing towards the fabric and the coal dust that had been thrown at it. It blew the dust further and further back, and then blew the black figure back as well. My eyes focused on the black figure as it was forced back toward the left of my field of vision until it was completely out of sight.

As my eyes turned very slowly back toward the fabric, I was grieving because I thought the coal dust had ruined it. However, to my amazement, the fabric was perfect. In answer to that thought, the voice said, "Satan cannot destroy the righteous acts of the saints."

Immediately, the words of Revelation 19:6-8 came to mind:

Hallelujah!
For our Lord God Almighty reigns.
Let us rejoice and be glad and give Him glory!
For the wedding of the Lamb has come,
And His bride has made herself ready.
Fine linen, bright and clean, was given her to wear.
(Fine linen stands for the righteous acts of the saints)."

I understood that the mighty wind was the Holy Spirit. I also understood that the arms holding the scroll of fabric in the bottom left corner were the arms of Jesus Christ. They were flesh; the angels were spirit.

Reflection questions

1. What do you see in your own lifestyle that is not pleasing to the Holy Spirit? In which area are you most in need of His purifying fire?
2. Has anyone spoken a prophetic word to you that you disregarded because they were words of correction you did not want to receive?

Will you pray with me?

May I suggest offering up a simple prayer for a fresh infilling of the Holy Spirit?

"Father, please forgive me, for I have sinned in the following ways: _____. I ask that You cleanse me with the blood of Jesus, according to Your Word. Please don't leave me as I am, but change me, Lord, and fill me to overflowing with the Holy Spirit, for Your glory and Your purposes. In Jesus' name, I pray. Amen!"

Memorization verse

Galatians 5:16 (NASB), "For I say, walk by the Spirit, and you will not carry out the desire of the flesh."

SMALL GROUP DISCUSSION QUESTIONS

Note to discussion leaders: Before proceeding to the discussion questions, it is helpful to begin by asking the women if there was some point in the assigned chapter that they identified with or that was new to them. If time allows, you may also want to discuss the reflection questions listed at the end of the chapter.

1. Have you ever prayed to be filled with the Holy Spirit? Are you afraid of what He would have you do? (As a new believer, I was afraid God would have me stand on Main Street and preach the gospel.)
2. As an immature believer, I pursued the gifts and power of the Spirit while not growing in the fruit of the Spirit, with disastrous results. Can you relate to this? (Please read 1 Corinthians 13:1-2; 14:1.)
3. Have you seen through this lesson how essential unity is, in order for the church to become the glorious bride for whom Christ is returning? Have you separated yourself from believers in other denominations or circles (i.e., Catholics vs. non-Catholics, charismatic vs. non-charismatic) because of different views? How does God see these differences, if all true believers are "in Christ"?

Part Two

Our Families

Chapter 9 ❧

Families in Crisis: A Home Out of Order

"UNLESS THE LORD builds the house, its builders labor in vain" (Ps. 127:1). In Scripture, the word *house* is "symbolic of the life of an individual or a family."[1] The first eight chapters covered aspects of our inner lives: allowing God to tear down the "houses" that we've built and surrendering to His will for our lives. We are now moving into the second part of this book, which focuses on the power we have as believers to stop generational strongholds and affect our families and future generations for good.

We know what a stronghold is: a strongly held belief or attitude that is contrary to the truth of God's Word, which Satan uses to enslave us to sin. A generational stronghold, then, is a stronghold that is passed from one generation to the next. We're going to be examining addictions and bondage to sin. I'll be referring to alcoholism because that is part of my family history. Consider what issue has been plaguing your family over the generations. For many it is divorce, perhaps coming out of a generational stronghold of bitterness. For others, it may be an addiction to food, producing obesity. Be willing to face the truth about your family in order to break through the denial that you (and your family members) have engaged in.

I mentioned earlier that I grew up in a family that had been devastated by alcoholism and that my brothers and I were deeply affected by that.

Years later, when we found out our teenage son had been using drugs (I say this with his permission), I thought I would have a complete emotional breakdown. Instead, I repented. The Holy Spirit spoke words of correction to me, and I began taking responsibility for my contribution to my family's problems. I want to share with you what He has taught me about generational strongholds and their role in dysfunctional families.

God did not design the family to be dysfunctional. Something that is dysfunctional is not functioning according to its design. Therefore, the term *dysfunctional family* refers to any family that is not functioning according to *God's design.* Many people say, "Every family is dysfunctional." That belief is very convenient, however, because it relieves us of any responsibility to change. Healthy family dynamics do exist; imperfection is not dysfunction. There is a huge difference between being a member of an imperfect family made up of imperfect people and being part of a dysfunctional family. I should know . . . I've lived in both. In this chapter, we will be looking at extreme cases of dysfunction where one or more family members have a life-controlling problem. Dysfunction produces very visible symptoms: continual crises and constant conflict, addictions, and codependency.

Continual crises and constant conflict

In a dysfunctional family, instead of peace or harmony in the home, there is drama. Conflict is normal, and when we seek biblical resolution, conflict can actually deepen our level of closeness and trust for one another. In a dysfunctional family, however, there is constant conflict with no resolution. Instead, family members "sweep things under the rug," allowing anger and resentment to fester, which only leads to more conflict. No repentance, restitution, or reconciliation occurs. If we came out of a dysfunctional family, crisis and conflict feel normal to us, and if we don't have it, we will make choices that create it. We won't realize we're doing that, and in fact, will believe we are acting to resolve problems. You can see, then, how conflict as a way of life would be generational, with the modeled attitudes and behavior of the parents being passed on to the children. Beliefs generate behaviors; generational strongholds produce generational behaviors.

Alcoholism and other addictions

We want to look at alcoholism and other addictions since they are so prevalent in our culture and even within the body of Christ. We will see that the biblical term for *addiction* is bondage or slavery to sin. Other addictions include workaholism. If a man is so obsessed with working that he has no time for his children, do they care whether their dad is at the bar or at the office? No, I don't think they do. We hear about "rage-aholics." If a parent habitually goes into rages, the children walk around on "eggshells" and develop deep-seated fear and anxiety because they just don't know what's going to trigger that rage. We also see compulsive credit card spending throwing families into financial crises. This too is an addiction.

Addictions are the result of strongholds. Strongholds are the "root" and the addictions (or destructive behaviors) are the "fruit." Addictions always include a stronghold of rebellion but may also involve shame and an inability to trust God, often because of childhood experiences. If a woman was belittled, shamed, or abused as a child by an authority figure, she often reacts in rebellion against authority as she gets older. The Lord put on my heart that "rebellion is the seedbed of all addictions," and I hope that by the end of this chapter you will know the full meaning of that statement.

Codependency

Codependency is a secular term describing behavior that is symptomatic of dysfunctional families, and in biblical terms, we would call it a stronghold of idolatry. It is a stronghold because it stems from the false belief that one's well-being is dependent on the choices, actions, and emotions of someone else rather than on one's own relationship with God (Proverbs 3:5-6). It is idolatry because it makes another person the center or focus of one's life. Let me make this personal. This spiritual condition causes us to be obsessed with the behavior of others, and what we consider to be their life-controlling problem, instead of looking at ourselves. The irony is that, as codependent people, we also have a life-controlling problem but are in so much denial that we can't see it. The stronghold of self-deception (denial) is characterized by self-pity, an innocent victim mentality, and the false belief that we know best. As God's Word tells us, "arrogance [is] like the evil of idolatry" (1 Sam. 15:23 NIV). Jesus said, "First take the plank out of your eye, and then you will see clearly to remove the speck from your brother's eye" (Luke 6:42).

God's Word on generational strongholds

We want to see what God's Word has to say on the subject of generational strongholds, and we will do that by examining the familiar passage on the Ten Commandments found in Exodus 20:1-17. These were given to the Israelites after Moses led them out of slavery in Egypt. I love the Old Testament! I believe in the literal interpretation of those great stories, but I also see them as a "flannel graph" that provides pictures of spiritual applications for us today.

Verses 1-2: "And God spoke all these words: I am the Lord your God, who brought you out of Egypt, out of the land of slavery." We can say that Moses leading Israel out of slavery in Egypt is a picture of Christ leading us out of slavery to sin through our union with Him. It's a great picture!

Verse 3: "You shall have no other gods before me." Do you recall the statement I made in Chapter 1: All sin is meeting our own needs in our own way, independently of God?[2] Whoever or whatever we turn to in order to meet our needs is our "god." You can see, then, how this verse applies to all of us at various times and to varying degrees. We are to have no other gods before Him, and yet we do, don't we?

Verse 4: "You shall not make for yourselves an idol in the form of anything in heaven above or on the earth beneath or in the waters below." An idol can be a person or object; it can be *anything*. It can be material possessions, but it can also be an obsession with a person. We've all heard of "relationship addictions," where individuals seek their happiness, comfort, and identity from their relationship with another person. That other person becomes an idol. It is whoever or whatever we give our lives to, or turn to for comfort, instead of turning to God the Father. Remember, Jesus died for our sins to bring us into relationship with the Father. He is to be the source of all comfort.

One day the Lord spoke to my heart: "Why do you look to others for what I intend to give you?" Is that speaking of codependency? Yes!

Is that speaking of idolatry? Yes! Now let's read the sobering words of verses 5-6:

> You shall not bow down to them or worship them; for I, the Lord your God, am a jealous God, punishing the children for the sins of the fathers to the third and fourth generations of those who hate me but showing love to a thousand generations of those who love me and keep my commandments.

This verse tells us that the Lord is a jealous God: He is jealous of our affections. He wants us to turn to Him, not to anyone or anything else. In fact, He demands it. He is worthy of our whole-hearted devotion and affection, and yet this requirement is for our sakes as well. He loves us and is the only One Who can satisfy our deepest needs. But the passage goes on to say, "punishing the children for the sins of the fathers. . . ." It sounds as though God is punishing innocent children for the sins of their fathers. We can see that sin has generational implications; however, children are not punished for their parents' sins. Instead, their lives are deeply affected by their parents' sins, as when an infant is born of a drug-addicted mother and is born addicted himself.

Here is where I believe that the King James Version captures the meaning more clearly: "visiting the iniquity of the fathers upon the children. . . ." Exodus 20:5 is not saying that an *innocent* child will be punished for the sins of the parent, but rather, that the children will generally commit the same sins as the parent. It is partly because of modeled behavior, but we must also realize that the "root" of the child—physically, emotionally, and spiritually—is in the parent. The parents are the root; the children are the fruit of the union of the mother and father. We see that genetically; and we see that emotionally, as a parent's temperament, fears, and anxieties can be passed on to the child. This is not just an outward influence; a spiritual dimension is involved, as shown in this passage. We see it at work in adopted children and in children who were separated from their fathers since birth, where they have the same sinful tendencies (such as alcoholism and addictions). I've seen teenagers who are just like the fathers they never knew.

While we are not responsible for the choices our children make as they get older, we are responsible for what we have sown into their lives. When we found out our son had been using drugs, I blamed my husband since I saw him as the role model. But the Lord showed me that I had sown seeds of rebellion into our children (my daughter also) by refusing to submit or yield to my husband's leadership in the home. What I've learned is that mothers are actually the role model for teaching the children how to submit to all authority, as our children observe how we submit to our husbands' God-ordained leadership in the home. Considering what is going on in our culture, that's a scary thought, isn't it? For twenty years of my marriage, I had refused to do that and we certainly lived a dysfunctional life, believe me.

When I realized what I had done, and that I did not have the power to undo the damage—to "un-sow" that seed—I cried out to God in deep repentance. One of many wonderful things I learned from this experience is that generational strongholds and resulting destructive behaviors can be broken through the process of repentance—our repentance! We always want someone else to repent, but the Lord showed me that through *my* repentance, He would move on my behalf to do what I could not do for myself: bring healing to my children. He spoke to me through Psalm 81:13-14, the context of which is repentance and restoration, exactly what I needed: "If my people would but listen to me, if [they] would follow my ways, how quickly would I subdue their enemies and turn my hand against their foes!"

Do you see what the Lord is saying here? If I would repent and do things His way instead of what I thought was right (human reasoning), He would move on my behalf. Who is our enemy? Ephesians 6:12 tells us our struggle is "not against flesh and blood," which means that people are not the enemy. We tend to think they are, but in reality, it is "the powers of this dark world." Satan is our enemy. And what is his agenda? It is to steal, kill, and destroy (John 10:10). He wants to wreck our lives and destroy our families.

This is an incentive for us to repent because repentance always brings deliverance. The NIV Study Bible makes the following comment on verse 5: "*of those who hate me.* Those Israelites who blatantly violate God's covenant and show that they reject the Lord as their king will bring down judgment on themselves and their households."[3] To love the Lord is to obey Him (John 14:15); "to reject the Lord as [our] King" is to refuse to submit to His authority, and it is as though we hate Him. As God's people, we can apply this to ourselves. No believer is going to say he hates God, but that's what disobedience is equated with. Satan wants to deceive us into believing we can rebel against God's authority without paying the consequences, but that is a lie—and a very destructive one. Jesus cancelled the curse of the law (Galatians 3:13; Colossians 2:13-14), but not the consequences of disobedience. We reap what we sow (Galatians 6:7). Here, as the children grow older, they generally repeat the modeled behavior of the parents and are punished for committing the same sins as their parents before them. *The key here is the sin of rebellion.*

A root of rebellion

In this chapter, we will see the connection between rebellion and addictions. We will see that we are in a spiritual battle for the family, and that Satan's tactics haven't changed. Just as he deceived and incited Eve to rebel against the Lord's instructions, so he continues to lure us into self-destruction.

God's Word has much to say about rebellion against His authority and the dire consequences of engaging in such behavior. This revelation brought a major breakthrough in my life, second only to tearing out a root of bitterness. Romans 13:1-2 speaks of submitting to all rightful authority:

Everyone must submit himself to the governing authorities, for there is no authority except that which God has established. The authorities that exist have been established by God. Consequently, he who rebels against the authority is rebelling against what God has instituted, and those who do so will bring judgment on themselves.

We see, then, that rebellion against God-ordained authority is rebellion against God. "Consequently, [those] who rebel against the authority . . . will bring judgment on themselves." The judgment we bring on ourselves comes in the form of consequences. We are our own worst enemy, yet many of us have blamed God for the pain in our lives, seeing Him as harsh and punitive. Instead, we need to understand that God has put a spiritual law into motion: we reap what we sow. We see in the above passage that if we rebel against any rightful authority—school officials and teachers, civil laws (speed limits!), etc., we are actually rebelling against God. So the Lord uses the consequences *of our own actions* to bring us to repentance and teach us His ways. Why? Because He loves us! He knows that the only place of peace and blessing is in submission to His will and His ways.

Scripture tells us in First Samuel 15 that King Saul had disobeyed the Lord's command, and instead, relied on his own human reasoning. The prophet Samuel confronted King Saul with these words: "For rebellion is as the sin of witchcraft . . . " (verse 23 KJV). The New International Version uses the word *divination* instead of *witchcraft*, but the King James Version speaks more clearly to me here. I hope you know that anyone who practices witchcraft is opening up his or her life to demonic activity. That is spiritual darkness and you don't want to go there! And yet, "rebellion is as the sin of witchcraft . . . " (verse 23 KJV). Witchcraft is Satan's domain; it is spiritual darkness. In the same way, rebellion gives Satan legal access to our lives and families, just as witchcraft would. Through rebellion, we give Satan a foothold, even as with unresolved anger (Ephesians 4:27).

When you, as a believer, are in rebellion against authority, you are *operating* in Satan's domain of spiritual darkness, contrary to your position in Christ (Colossians 1:13). James 4:7 makes this connection: "Submit yourselves, then, to God. Resist the devil, and he will flee from you." This is the essence of spiritual warfare because submission to the will of God brings deliverance from the enemy. Yet we cannot deceive ourselves into believing that we're submitting to God if we are not submitting to God-ordained authority. We're going to be studying "God's design for marriage" in Chapter 10, and we'll see that God has given the husband the authority and leadership in the home. If a wife rejects her husband's position, she will bring judgment on herself.

God's umbrella of protection

God has provided authority as a covering of protection against the demonic realm. We, as parents, are a covering for our children. The consequences of rebellion, therefore, are very serious. I want you to picture a large umbrella, representing God-ordained authority. Since authority is God's will, imagine a shaft of light coming down from inside the umbrella. When we walk in submission to authority, we walk in the light. Outside the perimeter of the umbrella, which would represent rebellion against God-ordained authority, is spiritual darkness. It is Satan's domain. Psalm 3:3 tells us, "But you are a shield around me, O Lord. . . ." The NIV Study Bible comments: "One's king is his shield."[4] When we submit to God and all God-ordained authority, He is our shield. Therefore, I want you to view authority as God's umbrella of protection. *Authority = God's will = God's umbrella of protection.*

With this in mind, I want to create another word picture for you. I mentioned above that the husband's position of authority is God-ordained; therefore, it is under this umbrella. However, his behavior and performance may not be; the husband himself may have stepped out from under authority into rebellion. Therefore, picture that umbrella with the husband outside the perimeter, wandering around in spiritual darkness. (Note: This is a picture of behavior, not identity. In the spiritual realm, believers have already been delivered from the domain of darkness (Colossians 1:13), but may act as though they have not.)

In this case, do you think that the solution for the wife would be to rebel against her husband's position of authority, thus stepping out from under God's umbrella? She would also be moving into the spiritual darkness of rebellion. If the mother and father are "out there" in rebellion, where are the children? They will naturally follow their parents into rebellion. In effect, the parents are laying their children wide open to demonic attack. Instead, since the husband's position of authority remains under God's umbrella, the wife can choose to submit to her husband's position rather than react to his behavior, as John Wesley said, "in everything that is not contrary to any command of God."[5]

God impressed on my heart that I was not to wait for someone else (my husband) to obey Him before I obeyed Him. Instead, I had to begin to submit to my husband's position of authority about four years before God brought my husband to repentance. Apart from the power of the Holy Spirit, I could not have done this. "With [woman] this is impossible, but with God all things are possible" (Matt. 19:26)! I learned that if we would yield to our husbands' leadership, God Himself would move on our behalf to heal our families. Friend, God has given us so much power and influence to affect our families for good, but the enemy has deceived us and caused us to rebel against the very thing that God designed for our protection: the husband's position of authority.

Getting to the root of the problem

Codependency may be a coping mechanism developed in childhood. For example, perhaps one of the parents had an addiction such as gambling or drinking or was codependent. What I mean is this: let's say that the father had a drinking problem and the mother was codependent because she was obsessed with the father's drinking. She was fearful of the consequences of his drinking and focused all of her attention on how much he drank, what he was doing, and how much money he was spending. In the process, she neglected the children emotionally. Ultimately, the father was emotionally absent because of his drinking; the mother was emotionally absent because of her obsession with her husband's drinking. Therefore, the children grow up believing, "If I don't take care of myself, no one else will." And that cycle continues, generation after generation.

Often when our loved ones refuse to take on their responsibilities, we feel compelled to take them on, or fix their problems, in order to avoid a crisis (the kind of crisis that needs to happen, which is the consequences of their actions). *"Enabling" is taking on the responsibilities of others, or trying to solve their problems, thus enabling them to continue in their addictive or destructive behavior.*

Mike Quarles, former co-director of Freedom In Christ Recovery Ministry along with his wife, Julia, said, "If you want to raise an alcoholic or a drug addict, never let them suffer the consequences of their actions."[6] We've studied Hebrews 12:5-6, which speaks of the Lord disciplining us as sons. God uses consequences to bring us to repentance and teach us His ways. It is idolatry when we do not allow God to teach our children His ways; we're actually putting them before God.

When we interfere with that process, if we "bail them out" (often, literally), they don't suffer the consequences—we do. There is no motivation to change their behavior; therefore, it gets worse. God then increases the severity of the consequences to accomplish His purposes. We wonder why things are getting worse and why God is not answering our prayers. In reality, *we are responsible for the escalation of the situation.* Until our loved ones repent (change their minds concerning their sin), their behavior will not change. We can waste years of our lives trying to change them. You and I know that doesn't work. As long as we are in control, God steps back and lets us have our way until we admit *our guilt*: we are in rebellion against God's authority. We must see that codependent behavior, which is idolatry, could not exist without the sin of rebellion.

We think we're expressing love; we think we're being merciful, when in reality what we are doing is practicing enabling. *Enabling is a distorted view of God's mercy.* The Greek word for *mercy* (*eleeo*) means "to help the afflicted, bring help to the wretched." Mercy is an attribute of God, which He administers directly or indirectly through us by the power of the Holy Spirit. God extends His mercy to all, but those in rebellion unknowingly reject it. (They are deceived because they are not walking in the light, under God's umbrella of authority). Therefore, God withholds the fullest extent of His mercy until they repent. God tells us in Hosea 5:2, 15, "I will discipline all of [the rebels]. . . . Then I will go back to my place until they admit their guilt. And they will seek my face; in their misery they will earnestly seek me" (amplification added).

I lived that out, and I can remember seeking the Lord in my misery, finally willing to face the truth about myself at any cost. Can you at all relate? The fullest extent of God's mercy comes when we repent. What we are showing through enabling is not mercy but fear—fear of what might happen if we don't intervene, instead of entrusting our loved ones to God's care and allowing them to suffer the consequences of their actions. I know what that fear is like. I became terrified when I found out about my son's drug use (again, I say this with his permission). I had a family history of alcoholism and chemical addiction. My youngest brother had a drug problem as a teenager and committed suicide at the age of twenty-six. Can you imagine how frightened I felt for my son? But I had to face the reality that my ways had not protected him, and I had to do things God's way.

God's Solution

What is God's solution for codependency and addictions that come out of the generational stronghold of rebellion? It is a simple answer but one that will require a radical change in our attitudes: *submit to all God-ordained authority, beginning in the home.*

The Lord can use our submission to authority to tear down a stronghold of rebellion in our families. Second Corinthians 10:4-5 tells us, "The weapons we fight with are not the weapons of the world. On the contrary, they have divine power to demolish strongholds." What is contrary to rebellion? Submission to authority. God uses our submission like an instrument, a "divine weapon," to tear down the rebellion in our families, even extending to our adult children. *This is the only way to bring restoration to our families—and it begins with us.* At the time the Lord was dealing with me about rebellion, I held little hope for my marriage. The promise of Isaiah 54:13, in the context of repentance and restoration, motivated me to obey as the Lord spoke to my heart: "Your sons will be taught by the Lord, and great will be your children's peace."

The Lord is raising up an army of women who will choose to lay down their wills and their lives—not to a man but to God—because He alone can heal their children and restore their families.

Reflection questions

1. I want you to see how important forgiveness is in this process. If we are bound by any sinful habit, we cannot get free except by the grace of God, Who will not give it without our willingness to forgive. What price are you paying for your refusal to forgive?
2. Can you look back over your life and see where the painful circumstances of your life were caused by your own rebellion, as you stepped out from under God's umbrella of protection?

Will you pray with me?

"Heavenly Father, we are so thankful that You have revealed to us both the problem and the solution. Lord, I pray that You would work into our hearts the ways in which we need to repent. Let us see, Lord, where we are rebelling against authority, where we are resisting God-ordained leadership. And so, Father, we trust that You are going to begin that work even now, to tear down a stronghold of rebellion in us, in our families, and in the generations that follow, for Your glory and Your purposes. In Jesus' name, we pray. Amen!"

Memorization verse

Romans 13:2, "Consequently, he who rebels against the authority is rebelling against what God has instituted, and those who do so will bring judgment on themselves."

SMALL GROUP DISCUSSION QUESTIONS

Note to discussion leaders: Before proceeding to the discussion questions, it is helpful to begin by asking the women if there was some point in the assigned chapter that they identified with or that was new to them. If time allows, you may also want to discuss the reflection questions listed at the end of the chapter.

1. Whose lives are you too involved in, always trying to "fix" their problems and straighten them out? Could it be your husband or your older children? What actions have you taken and what problems have you caused as a result?
2. Do you recognize addictions and/or codependency in your birth family? Do you see these traits in yourself, and if so, are you passing generational strongholds on to your children?
3. True brokenness does not come as a result of the pain others have caused us, but rather from a revelation of the pain we have caused others. What pain have you caused and what damage have you done to others, especially your children?

Chapter 10 ❧

God's Design for Marriage

WE LIVE IN a post-Christian era, which means our culture is no longer driven by Christian values. The passage in Ephesians that we'll review in this chapter may appear to you to be outdated and unrealistic, meant for another time. However, God's Word is eternal and His design for marriage has not changed. We will see that marriage is a reflection of the relationship between Jesus Christ and His bride, the church, according to Ephesians 5. Since that relationship has not changed in 2,000 years, neither has the pattern for marriage.

This chapter is the centerpiece of the *Weatherproof Your Home* teaching. Every biblical principle that I've presented to you up to this point has been designed to prepare you mentally, emotionally, and spiritually to embrace the truth of God's Word concerning marriage. The two remaining chapters will flow out of this one: *Ministry Begins at Home* and *It's Not About Us*. God is restoring our families so that we can be true ministers of reconciliation to lost and hurting people.

Let's take a verse-by-verse look at Ephesians 5:21-33, and actually, I want to start with the last verse (verse 33): "However, each one of you [husbands] also must love his wife as he loves himself, and the wife must respect her husband." That does not mean that a husband is not required to *respect* his wife (1 Peter 3:7), or that a wife is not required to *love* her husband (Titus 2:4). Rather, it alludes to the fact that God has "wired" men to need respect; He has "wired" women to need love. Treating our husbands with respect can heal them of their past wounds, which in turn can enable them to love us in a way that heals us. Therefore, treating our husbands with disrespect is another form of self-defeating behavior.

Keeping in mind how we have failed our husbands, let us *humbly* move on to defining the word *submit* as shown in Ephesians 5:21-24: "Submit to one another out of reverence for Christ. Wives, submit to your husbands as to the Lord. For the husband is the head of the wife as Christ is the head of the church, his body, of which he is the Savior. Now, as the church submits to Christ, so also wives should submit to their husbands in everything."

Generally, women (and men) who don't want to accept the biblical principle of the husband's leadership in the home immediately focus on verse 21: "Submit to one another out of reverence for Christ." We will see from a study of the entire passage that the wife and husband do indeed submit to one another, but they do so in different ways. I wish I could recall the name of the teacher who first explained it in this way so I could properly credit him or her. This teacher wisely pointed out that the husband is to submit to his wife's *need,* while the wife is to submit to her husband's *lead.*

Let me emphasize that we must define our terms according to God's Word, not as the world defines them. According to John MacArthur, the Greek word for *submit (hupotasso),* "is not in the original text of verse 22 but is implied from its usage in verse 21. *Hupotasso* refers to a functional lining up and in no way implies a difference in essence."[1] The Greek lexicon defines it as "a Greek military term meaning 'to arrange in a military fashion under the command of a leader. In non-military use, it was a voluntary attitude of giving in, cooperating, assuming responsibility, and carrying a burden." In regard to our role as wives, what will that look like in its practical application? Let me clearly state what biblical submission is—and what it is not.

It is not domination: Biblical submission is something that can only be practiced willingly by the wife. As soon as it is coerced or demanded, it becomes domination. That is the world's definition of submission, but it is not God's.

It is not passivity: Submission is not weak or passive, but rather, it is strength under God's control. It is taking responsibility for our own lives and decisions. When we stand before Christ, we will stand alone. Therefore, we cannot avoid our responsibilities in the name of submission. A woman can't commit a wrong, such as watching pornography at her husband's request, and then justify it by saying she was just being submissive to her husband. Have you believed the lie that God's Word is telling us that no matter what our husbands do (or tell us to do), we are to obey? Biblical submission has biblical boundaries. We would never be led by the Spirit of God to do anything that contradicts the Word of God. Therefore, there may be times when we must respectfully decline to do what our husbands have asked or demanded.

It is never accepting abuse: In fact, the wife has a moral obligation to remove herself and her children from an abusive environment. It is an act of emotional abuse to allow children to witness and be exposed to that kind of behavior. Daughters will grow up believing that is how they are to be treated; sons will learn to disrespect women and may even demonstrate abusive behavior toward them later in life. Along with physical abuse, I want to include here the threat of violence. Wives are not to be terrorized by obsessed and controlling husbands, who may in fact be mentally ill.

Never confuse fear with submission. I want to repeat: submission is strength under God's control. When we respect our husbands' position of authority, we are walking in the light of God's Word and will have the spiritual discernment to know when they have crossed a boundary and what God wants us to do about it. Abuse is not only a sin but a crime as well, and God has instituted civil and church authority for our protection.

What is biblical submission?

What these points tell us, then, is that biblical submission has biblical boundaries. It is to be a mirror image of the church's relationship to Christ. Submission is Spirit-led and Spirit-empowered respect for the husband's leadership in the home, which is based on his God-given position, not his performance. Submission is seeking to do those things that build up and encourage our husbands, allowing them to view themselves as loved, respected, and significant.

The problem is that sometimes we don't *want* them to feel loved, respected, and significant! So, for many of us, this will require a radical shift in thinking. We must begin to treat our husbands with respect *unconditionally*, in the same way that we are taught as Christians to love unconditionally. This requires that we *respond* out of the character of Christ within us (the fruit of the Spirit), rather than *react* to their behavior. I think you'll agree that most men know when they don't "deserve" respect, and our godly behavior will humble them and allow the Holy Spirit to convict them of their sin.

When our husbands are healed, then they can love. If they have not been healed in that way, we need to take the first step and begin the process of mutual healing. I finally became more concerned about being the "love-er" than the "love-ee." I saw that I had retaliated and hurt my husband in so many ways and to such a degree that I finally grieved more over the pain I had caused him than over the pain he had caused me. That's when I became willing to take that first step.

We're like hamsters on an exercise wheel, going round and round. No one wants to be the first one to get off that treadmill. You say, "I'll get off when he gets off." He says, "I'll get off when she gets off." For twenty-five years of our marriage, my husband and I went "round and round" with each other. Remember: the definition of insanity is doing the same things over and over again, expecting the outcome to change!

Defining male headship

I began my college education at the age of forty-nine, and while researching for a paper on "male headship" in the home (which refers to the husband's position as "head" of the wife in Ephesians 5:23), I learned that there is a heated debate over the meaning of that one word. At the heart of the controversy was the meaning of the Greek term *kephale* (head), as used by the apostle Paul in this passage: "For the husband is the head of the wife as Christ is the head of the church, his body, of which he is the Savior. Now as the church submits to Christ, so also wives should submit to their husbands in everything" (Eph. 5:22-23).

126

Some theologians are convinced that *kephale* here means "source," while others view the word as a metaphor for authority.[2] However, we see that the meaning is made clear by its usage in this passage: the husband is the "head" of his wife *in the same way* that Christ is the "head" of the church. In that sense, it is both "authority" *and* "source." Scripture tells us that Jesus is our Authority: "Then Jesus came to them and said, 'All authority in heaven and on earth has been given to me'" (Matt. 28:18). God's Word also tells us that Jesus is to be our Source: "His divine power has given us everything we need for life and godliness through our knowledge of him who called us by his own glory and goodness" (2 Peter 1:3).

Just as Christ is the source and provider for the church, so also the husband is responsible to provide for his wife. Just as Christ leads and has authority over the church, so the husband leads and has authority over the wife, but not for his own advantage. Authority is necessary to lead; even the world knows that. The husband's example is Christ as Servant-leader: "Husbands, love your wives, just as Christ loved the church and gave himself up for her. . . . In this same way, husbands ought to love their wives as their own bodies. . . ." (verses 25, 28). Husbands have been given the position of authority because they have been given the responsibility of laying down their lives in love and devotion for their wives. *The one with the authority is the one with the responsibility.*

Based on the model of Christ and the church, the husband is Christ's representative in the family and is held accountable before God for the condition of the family (1 Timothy 3:5). He is to treat his wife with gentleness and respect (1 Peter 3:7); otherwise, his prayers will be hindered. The Greek word for *hindered* is *ekkopto* and means to "cut off." In practical terms, it could mean that if a husband overburdens his wife by expecting her to maintain the home, spend her evenings helping the children with their homework, *and* work full-time outside the home so that he can drive a new truck—his prayers will be "cut off" from the Lord.

Not only is the husband responsible for the physical protection of his wife, but his position of authority also functions as a spiritual covering of protection against the demonic realm, even as Christ is the covering of protection over the church. Lest you think this has nothing to do with the spiritual realm, let's review what we learned in *Chapter 9: Families in Crisis*: "Submit yourselves, then, to God. Resist the devil and he will flee from you" (James 4:7). If we do not submit to established positions of authority, we are *not* submitting to God (Romans 13:1-2), and Satan is under no legal obligation to flee. When we reject our husbands' "headship," we move out from under God's umbrella of protection into spiritual darkness, contrary to our spiritual position in Christ (Colossians 1:13). Consequently, our lives become full of pain and difficulty. Then what do we do? We blame our husbands!

Some women say, "My husband is passive; he won't lead." After twenty-five years of marriage, I had programmed my husband to be passive. I was controlling and domineering, and it did not pay him to make a decision. And I'm not alone. So many of us have stripped our husbands of their roles. But when I got out of God's way, He began to teach my husband how to lead. And though my husband was very passive in the past, he is a very strong leader in our home today.

If the wife rebels against her husband's authority, it may be because the husband is not submitting to her needs. (The wife is to submit to her husband's *lead*; the husband is to submit to his wife's *need*).[3] This is the way in which we are to submit one to another: we submit to our roles and responsibilities. However, if the husband is not fulfilling his role, the wife's rebellion is not the answer. When we submit "as unto the Lord," God moves on our behalf: "If my people would but listen to me, if [they] would follow my ways, how quickly would I subdue their enemies and turn hand against their foes" (Ps. 81:13-14).

The husband's authority and the wife's submission are equally valuable and essential functions within God's design for marriage. They are for the benefit of the wife, for the protection of the children, and for the preservation of the family.

The anointing

Another biblical term we need to define is the "anointing" of God. When something was anointed in the Old Testament, it was consecrated and set apart for God's purposes. "Christ" means "the Anointed One." We find in Luke 4 that when Jesus began His ministry, He quoted from Isaiah 61:1, which follows in its entirety: "The Spirit of the Sovereign Lord is on me, because the Lord has anointed me to preach good news to the poor. He has sent me to bind up the brokenhearted, to proclaim freedom for the captives and release from darkness for the prisoners. . . ." John Wesley defines the anointing as "capacitating gifts and commissioning authority."[4]

All believers are anointed. First John 2:20 tells us, "But you have an anointing from the Holy One, and all of you know the truth." We are anointed because we are "in Christ," the Anointed One. Why have we been anointed? For what purpose have we been given capacitating gifts and commissioning authority? Ephesians 2:10 tells us, "For we are God's workmanship, created in Christ Jesus to do good works, which God prepared in advance for us to do." We see that we're only anointed to do the good works which "*God* prepared in advance for us to do," so it's vitally important that we know what those good works are. As I've stated previously, the Spirit of God will *never* contradict the Word of God. So it is to the Word of God that we must turn in order to find out what our roles and responsibilities are.

Understanding this concept of the anointing as it relates to the husband's headship is critical. I want to present biblical principles that will line up to show us what is being accomplished as we submit to our husbands' position of authority. In order to do that, I want to share two principles concerning the anointing. The first is: The anointing flows from the head down.

Oil symbolizes the Holy Spirit, so I want you to picture the power of the Holy Spirit being poured out like oil on the head. In Exodus 29:7, God told Moses to anoint and consecrate his brother, Aaron, as a priest: "Take the anointing oil and anoint him by pouring it on his head." This will tie in with Psalm 133:1-2, "How good and pleasant it is when brothers live together in unity! It is like precious oil poured on the head, running down on the beard, running down on Aaron's beard, down upon the collar of his robe."

These verses refer back to the passage in Exodus where God commanded Moses to take the anointing oil and pour it on Aaron's head. But this passage is also telling us that unity is like that anointing oil that flows down from the head. It runs down over Aaron's beard, down upon the collar of his robes, representing the natural flow of that anointing as it is poured out upon the head, running down upon the body. In the Ephesians 5 passage, the apostle Paul uses the analogy of the body to represent the church, with Christ as her head. The wife, then, is pictured as the body, with the husband as her head. Earlier, I stated that the Greek lexicon defines the word *submit* as a military term meaning to "arrange [line up] under." If the wife is "lined up under" her husband's *position of authority,* the anointing flows from Christ onto the husband as the head, over the wife as the body . . . and then where? The unity between husband and wife enables the flow of anointing to pour over the children. It's important to note that only the wife can produce unity, as she is the one to decide whether she will line up under her husband's leadership. If the wife refuses to yield to her husband's leadership, will the anointing of his headship flow over her life? No, it will not. Since the children generally follow the mother's modeled behavior into rebellion, will they choose to come under the father's anointing of headship? It's very unlikely.

When God first began to deal with me and teach me about this principle, my marriage was a shambles and I actually did not hold out much hope for it. When I learned, however, that my submission would enable God's anointing to flow down over my children, I became willing to do whatever God required—if it killed me! And it just about did . . . the part of me that needed to die: my will, my pride, my ego! But what woman among us would not be willing to lay down her life so that the anointing power of Almighty God would flow in the lives of her children?

The Lord is raising up an army of women who will choose to line up under their husbands' God-ordained position of leadership so that the anointing power of Almighty God will flow over their children.

I have prayed that you would receive a revelation of the anointing power of Christ coming down upon the husband's position of "headship." See also that even if the husband has stepped out from under Christ's authority into rebellion, his position of "headship" remains under the umbrella because it is God-ordained. The wife can submit to her husband's position of authority and remain under that covering, even though the husband has stepped out into rebellion. And to be sure,

God will give her discernment concerning safe boundaries. If you've grown up in a dysfunctional family, you probably have no clue about boundaries. But when you walk in the light, under authority, God will teach you about healthy boundaries, as He did for me.

God uses our submission as a spiritual weapon to tear down rebellion in us, in our husbands, and in our children. I also have to say that not every husband will respond and repent because they have free will. For a wife, however, submission is a "win-win" situation, because as she defers to her husband's leadership and trusts God to move on her behalf, He will deal with her husband. I believe that God takes it very seriously when one of his daughters submits to her husband out of love and reverence for Him. *He is her defender*! Please don't get the wrong idea: I do not mean that the wife should passively tolerate mistreatment while waiting for the Lord to do something. Part of the Lord's protection is to reveal to us exactly what steps *we* need to take and when we need to take them. I had an unsaved friend who had been in an abusive marriage for twenty years. Then she came to faith in Christ and began praying for direction. One Saturday morning shortly thereafter, the Lord alerted her to put her child and whatever belongings she could carry into her car—and leave!

I've seen two instances where women repented of their past rebellion and disrespect toward their husbands, and sought to treat their husbands with devotion and yield to their leadership. God saw their faithfulness and began to deal with their husbands. Those two men repeatedly refused to repent when confronted by church leadership, and God turned them over to their sin. Both men broke the marriage covenant and removed themselves from their marriages, but God's hand of protection was upon the wives and children. In time, those women went on to marry godly men who are completely devoted to them and their children. Again I say, submission is a win-win situation.

This brings me to the second important principle concerning the anointing: The anointing will destroy the yoke of the enemy. Let's look at Isaiah 10:27 (KJV): "the yoke [of the enemy] shall be destroyed because of the anointing" (amplification added). In context, Isaiah was speaking of Judah, the southern kingdom of the divided nation of Israel, which was being delivered from the Assyrians. But in a spiritual application to our lives, who is our enemy? Satan. The "yoke of the enemy," as it relates to us, is bondage or slavery to sin. Remember, Satan uses strongholds in our lives to enslave us to sin. What kind of sin? Rebellion, addictions, self-deception, bitterness, pride . . . and all the rest.

The above verse is taken from the King James Version, but the New International Version renders it this way: "The yoke will be broken because you have grown so fat." (Reading a couple different versions of the Bible can shed so much light on the meaning.) Here, I asked the Lord, "What does it mean that 'you have grown so fat'?" Interestingly, the word *fat* in Hebrew is *shemen*, and it is *oil for anointing*. The picture we need to see here is that the yoke of the enemy will be destroyed because we have grown so fat with the anointing. That anointing is the very life and virtue of Jesus Christ, growing so "fat" within us that the yoke of bondage can no longer hold us. Isn't that an awesome picture? That anointing is so important to us, but even more, we want that anointing to be on our children in order that they would also be so full of the life and virtue of Jesus Christ that they would break free of all bondage and live totally for Him.

Wives, get under your husbands' anointing of headship! Even an unbeliever is anointed to serve God in that position, just as secular government officials are God's servants (Romans 13:1-5). The unbelieving husband may be won over by the godly behavior of his wife (1 Peter 3:1). He is anointed as "head" and the wife is still to defer to his leadership.

The Lord is raising up an army of women who will line up under their husbands' God-ordained position of leadership so that the yoke of the enemy will be destroyed in their children's lives.

When wives reject their husbands' headship, they are actually rejecting God's spiritual covering of protection against the demonic realm, and they will teach their children to do the same. The wife is not anointed as head of the family. If you are trying to lead by controlling your husband, life will be very hard. *I liken it to a slow crawl over broken glass.* Proverbs 14:1 tells us: "The wise woman builds her house, but with her own hands the foolish one tears hers down."

Note to single/divorced women and moms: God has not abandoned you! Embrace the truth of God's Word concerning the husband's headship and repent of any past rebellion against authority. Come under all God-ordained authority, and Christ Himself will be your "Head:" your Provider, Protector, and Lover of your soul. "Your Maker is your husband, the Lord Almighty is His Name" (Isa. 54:5).

The model of Christ and the church

The marriage union is the only picture the world will ever see of the spiritual relationship between Christ and His bride, the church. What picture does your marriage present? Following, you will find a list of the four primary ways in which Christ relates to the church, and the ways that the church is to relate to Christ. That is the "template" for our relationship with our husbands. Please spend time reviewing these roles and their scriptural bases because we will focus on practical application of these principles in the next chapter. I've also included the Amplified Version of Ephesians 5:33. Please invite the Holy Spirit to teach you, comfort you, and renew your mind according to God's Word.

One last note before you begin: Fulfilling our God-given role and responsibilities in the home will *never* prevent us from fulfilling our destiny in Christ. In fact, the self-sacrifice required by submission will produce the character of Christ within us and equip us for all God has called us to be. Wives also need to be committed to their husbands' destiny in Christ, since we were created to be their helpmates (Genesis 2:18). If that sounds degrading to you, then you need to remember that the Holy Spirit was sent to us as a helpmate.

The marriage roles based on Ephesians 5:22-33

1. How does Christ relate to the church?
   a. Head of the church; authority and source (*kephale*) (verse 23)
   b. Servant-Leader: laid down His life (verse 25)
   c. Spiritual Leader: committed to her spiritual growth (verses 26-27)
   d. Provider and Protector: "feeds and cares for" (verses 28-29)

2. Therefore, what is the role of the husband?
   a. Head of the wife: authority and source
   b. Servant-leader: lay down his life for her
   c. Spiritual leader: committed to her spiritual growth
   d. Provider and protector: "feeds and cares for" his wife
3. How does the church relate to Christ?
   a. Looks to Him as her "first love" (verse 23; Rev. 2:4)
   b. Submits to His authority and follows Him (verse 24)
   c. Receives His provision and protection (verse 29)—a picture of grace (Eph. 2:8-9)
   d. Trusts in the Lord as her Savior (verse 23; Prov. 3:5-6)
4. Therefore, how is the wife to relate to her husband?
   a. Looks to her husband as her "first love"
   b. Submits to his authority and leadership
   c. Receives his provision and protection—as a picture of grace
   d. She trusts in the Lord as her Savior!

Defining the terms

I'm sure that when some of you read the following terms for responding to your husband, you will think, *You've got to be kidding me!* But treating your husband with respect, especially when he doesn't deserve it, will heal him and humble him, allowing the Holy Spirit to convict him of sin and teach him to love you sacrificially.

The Amplified Bible version of Ephesians 5:33 says, "Let the wife see that she respects and reverences her husband, [that she notices him, regards him, honors him, prefers him, venerates, and esteems him; and that she defers to him, praises him, and loves and admires him exceedingly]."[5]

The Merriam-Webster Dictionary defines:

Respect: "to consider deserving of high regard: esteem; to refrain from interfering with."[6]

Prefer: "to promote; to like better; to give priority."[7]

Venerate: "to regard with reverential respect or with admiring deference."[8]

Esteem: "to set a high value on; regard; respect, admire, revere."[9]

Defer: "to submit or yield to the opinion or wishes of another."[10]

Praise: "to express a favorable judgment of: commend."[11]

Love: "to feel a lover's passion, devotion, or tenderness for."[12]

Admire: "to regard with high esteem."[13]

To "submit" is a military term, and we are in a battle, are we not? We are in a battle for our families, and that battle is going to be won as we line up under our husbands' position of headship and leadership. Submission is not weakness but rather strength under God's control. We are warriors!

Reflection questions

1. If treating your husband with respect is what God uses to heal him of his past wounds, then the lack of it will cause his wounds to go deeper. What are some of the ways you've hurt your husband?
2. Where are you in embracing your husband's "headship" (your husband's position as servant-leader in your home)? Can you see the truth of God's Word shining through this principle? What will you do with what you've learned?

Will you pray with me?

"Heavenly Father, we have gone our own way and we've reaped so much havoc and destruction in our lives. We thank You for giving us Your Word and showing us that You have a specific design for marriage, that You have anointed our husbands' position, and that You provide deliverance as we walk in Your ways. In Jesus' Name we pray. Amen."

Memorization verse

Proverbs 14:1, "The wise woman builds her house, but with her own hand the foolish one tears hers down."

SMALL GROUP DISCUSSION QUESTIONS

Note to discussion leaders: Before proceeding to the discussion questions, it is helpful to begin by asking the women if there was some point in the assigned chapter that they identified with or that was new to them. If time allows, you may also want to discuss the reflection questions listed at the end of the chapter.

1. How has your childhood influenced your view of marriage? How has your mother's relationship with your father set a pattern in your own marriage?
2. Picture the anointing flowing from Christ onto your husband's position of authority. Have you "lined up under" your husband, so that the anointing power of the Holy Spirit is flowing in your life and onto your children? If not, what will you specifically do to change that?
3. Have you excused yourself from submission because your husband is not a believer, or if he is a believer, is not walking in obedience to God's Word? Besides changing your behavior, you will need to ask his forgiveness. How will you begin?

Chapter 11 ❧

Ministry Begins at Home

WE KNOW FROM our study of *Chapter 9: Families in Crisis* that a dysfunctional family is any family that is not functioning according to God's design. In extreme cases, these families are marked by constant conflict, continual crises, addictions and codependency. Often, family members are obsessed with the choices and behaviors of the addicted or self-destructive member, which allows them to deceive themselves about the changes that need to be made in their own lives. In the same way, I believe that the modern-day church, at least here in America, is a dysfunctional family. We have become so intent on "fixing" the world around us that we are oblivious to the strongholds and dysfunction in our own lives and families.

The church today looks no different from the world we are trying to save. The divorce rate is the same, our children are broken, and addictions are rampant. Yet we have refused to look at ourselves. Instead, we have thrown ourselves into more ministries as though that would excuse the sin in our lives. In Second Chronicles 7:14, we read, "if my people, who are called by my name, will humble themselves and pray and seek my face and turn from their wicked ways, then will I hear from heaven and will forgive their sin and will heal their land." What do we see in this passage that really brings about revival in a nation? It is the repentance of God's people!

The Holy Spirit is calling each of us to get our house in order. Do you recall our study of the Holy Spirit and the "big picture" of what He has come to do? He is preparing the bride for the coming of her Bridegroom, Jesus Christ. Jesus is not coming for a filthy, disheveled bride, but rather for a glorious bride. And so I believe that *something* will have to happen in order for us to become that bride without spot or blemish, not only in our position, but also in our practice—visibly holy before the world. I believe that the Holy Spirit is directing our attention back to the home. God cares very much about what goes on behind closed doors because that is where our true character is revealed. Speaking to you as one who has been guilty of this in the past, I am deeply concerned about those in church leadership and Christian service who use ministry as an excuse to neglect their God-given responsibilities in the home.

The body of Christ has given a higher priority to church growth than to family stability. Yet without family stability, there will be no true growth.

Many Christians serve in their churches or in Christian ministries. But if we could see behind closed doors, we would see in many cases that the men are not functioning as servant-leaders to their wives, and the wives are not respecting their husbands' position of authority. If all those whose homes were not in order would immediately remove themselves from ministry while they got that straightened out, how many people would be serving in our churches? Not many! Yet isn't that what we should do?

If ministry does not begin with our families, we will spend all of our time "putting out fires" in our own homes, while the world watches. This grieves me because I always speak to you as one who has failed. While serving on the local board of Christian Women's Club years ago, I attended a dinner meeting once a month. On those days, I left my children with a babysitter all day while I worked, then hurriedly fed them and left them with another babysitter—so I could minister to other women!

For many of us, ministry and the recognition or approval it brings medicates our emotional pain and allows us to escape the realities of a difficult marriage, or perhaps reveals an outright rebellion against our husbands' authority. Many of us are neglecting our responsibilities in the home, and especially our husbands, as we throw ourselves into more and more ministry at church. Yet we can be assured that no matter what committee we serve on, no matter what ministry we're involved in, it is merely for the praise of man if we are not first and foremost submitting to our husbands and putting them before all others.

Review of marriage roles

My purpose in Chapter 10 was to lay the scriptural foundation for God's design for marriage. This chapter will provide some practical application of those biblical principles. Let's review and expand on the marriage roles based on Ephesians 5:22-33. We can clearly see that the husband's role in the marriage relationship is to be modeled after Christ: he is to relate to his wife in the same way that Christ relates to His bride, the church. The wife's role is to be modeled after the church: she is to relate to her husband as the church relates to Christ. Let's take it verse by verse.

Verse 23: "For the husband is the head of the wife as Christ is the head of the church, His body, of which He is the Savior." Therefore, the husband is the head of the wife *in the same way* that Christ is the head of the church: both authority and source (Matthew 28:18; 2 Peter 1:3). The husband, of course, is not the wife's "savior," but her devotion to him is to be an outward expression of her devotion to Christ as her Savior and "first love" (Revelation 2:4). The wife's devotion to her husband, then, places him before all other *human* relationships.

Verse 24: "Now as the church submits to Christ, so also wives should submit to their husbands in everything." Therefore, in the same way that the church submits to Christ, the wife is to submit to her husband's authority and leadership, "in everything that is not contrary to any command of God."[1] When we submit to our husbands, we are actually placing our trust in Christ and walking in obedience to Him. Our husbands are human and they will fail us, even as we will fail them, but Jesus Christ will never fail us. He is our Rock and our Deliverer.

Verse 25: "Husbands, love your wives, just as Christ loved the church and gave Himself up for her. . . ." Therefore, the husband is a servant-leader: he is to lay down his life for his wife.

Verses 26-27: "to make her holy, cleansing her by the washing with water through the Word, and to present her to himself as a radiant church without spot or blemish, but holy and blameless." Therefore, the husband has the responsibility of spiritual leadership: he is to be committed to his wife's spiritual growth.

Verses 28-30: "In this same way, husbands ought to love their wives as their own bodies. He who loves his wife loves himself. After all, no one ever hated his own body, but he feeds and cares for it, just as Christ does the church—for we are members of his body." In the same spiritual sense that Christ is the head of the church, His body, so too the husband is the head and his wife is the body: "and the two will become one flesh" (verse 31). Just as Christ cares for His bride, the church (He provides for us and protects us) so too the husband is responsible to provide for and to protect his wife. Believers are recipients of the abundance of God's grace through our union with Christ. Therefore, the wife is to receive her husband's provision and protection as a picture of grace: "For it is by grace you have been saved, through faith—and this not from yourselves, it is the gift of God—not by works, so that no one can boast" (Eph. 2:8-9). When we receive and rely upon our husbands' provision, our marriages reflect the relationship between Christ and His bride. As we line up under our husbands' position of leadership, and as we wait on the Lord to provide through our husbands, we are trusting in God.

Marriage based on the model of Christ and the church as His bride, as presented in Ephesians 5, is a picture of the traditional family structure, with the husband as the head and provider of the family. Fifty years ago, when divorce was rare, the traditional family structure was the norm. Today, it is considered outdated and irrelevant to our times. Unfortunately, the results of embracing the modern world's standard are the same high divorce rate (or dead relationships), fatherless homes, wounded children, addictions . . . and the list goes on. Instead of taking care of each other's needs within the family, each member is trying to survive any way he or she can.

Let's get practical

It's time now to look at some practical application of the biblical principles we are learning. I always want to stress that this process of repentance and restoration is not about following rules, but about depending on the Holy Spirit in applying these principles, which serve as biblical boundaries for our lives.

Let's start with this one: *The one with the authority is the one with the responsibility.* Considering that a common theme in this book is "Mind Thy Own Business," why would I point out the husband's responsibilities? I am doing so because, unless we are aware of what the Lord has called husbands to be and do, we will either (a) take on their responsibilities ourselves, or (b) allow them to cross biblical boundaries in exercising their authority. By allowing men to violate biblical boundaries in marriage, we have given submission a bad name and undermined the authority of Scripture. Taking on our husbands' responsibilities is a form of disrespect because it treats them as children, and *enables* them to be irresponsible. God uses the pressures of their responsibilities to conform them to Christ and equip them for His call on their lives. We wouldn't want to interfere with that, would we?

Based on the model of Christ and the church, the husband stands as Christ's representative in the home and is held accountable before God for the condition of his family. The husband is accountable before God for the well-being of his family, which includes financial provision, discipline for the children, spiritual leadership, protection, and much more. "Here is a trustworthy saying: if anyone sets his heart on being an overseer, he desires a noble task. . . . He must manage his own family well and see that his children obey him with proper respect. (If anyone does not know how to manage his own family, how can he take care of God's church?)" (1 Tim. 3:1, 4-5).

To "manage" (NIV), or "to rule over" (KJV) is from the Greek word *proistemi*, which means to "superintend, to be a protector, to care for." Again, the husband's role in the marriage is the same as that of Christ in relation to the church, which is as authority and source, as both provider and protector. There is simply no way around this principle: the husband is the "overseer" of his family. It is exactly this kind of responsibility that equips a man to care for a church family or lead a ministry.

Based on the model of Christ and the church, the husband is responsible to provide for his wife and family. I've seen a calling to full-time ministry in a few men whose wives have become the main wage earner. As far as human reasoning goes, it made more sense for the wife's career to take precedence over the husband's because she made more money than her husband. Consequently, the husband became dependent on the wife instead of depending on God. In reality, if the wife would get out of the way by not taking on her husband's responsibilities, God would use the pressures of providing for the family to strengthen the husband's character and leadership gifts, as well as his dependence and faith in God.

I believe it is often the case that husbands are not flourishing in their callings because they are not first providing for their own families. "If anyone does not provide for his relatives, and especially for his immediate family, he has denied the faith and is worse that an unbeliever" (1 Tim. 5:8). That provision involves so much more than bringing home a paycheck. The Greek word for *provide* is *pronoeo,* and it means "to provide, think of beforehand; to take thought for, care for." It implies thoughtfully planning to meet the needs of another. In the same way that Jesus Christ looked down the corridor of time to determine and provide for everything we would need as His bride (2 Peter 1:3), so too the husband is called to plan ahead to anticipate the needs of his family, thus giving his wife a deep sense of security. Obviously, this is an overwhelming responsibility for the husband, one that should cause him to rely on the Lord in an ever increasing way.

God does not allow financial problems to come into our lives to encourage the wife to seek employment, but rather to encourage the husband to seek Him. This does not mean that wives should not be employed or add to the family income, but rather that God allows pressure in the area of finances to encourage husbands to rely upon Him. As husbands are called to provide, wives must be extremely frugal with household expenses when money is "tight," but husbands do not have the authority to insist that their wives find employment outside the home. It is the husband's responsibility to provide, and it is contrary to Scripture for the wife to abandon her role in order to take on his role. God uses the pressures of the husband's responsibilities to mold him into the man God created him to be and equip him for the calling God has placed on his life.

My purpose in stating the following is not to bring condemnation but to cause you to re-think your position. I must say that one of the deepest regrets of my life is working full time outside the home when my children were growing up. I had the privilege and responsibility to be at home, but I was not there. According to Titus 2:3-5, young wives have a responsibility to be "busy at home" and to care for their children. Older women may have the responsibility of caring for elderly parents, while not neglecting their husbands. This takes time, and I've learned that love is spelled T-I-M-E. One of my favorite verses is Ecclesiastes 4:6: "Better one handful with tranquility than two handfuls with toil and chasing after the wind." Does that strike a cord with you? Do you often feel that your life is full of "toil and chasing after the wind"? To me, that refers to the chaos which has been created in the home as the vital role of the wife and mother as homemaker has been degraded in our culture, and the lie has been perpetuated that two incomes are needed to "survive." That is not what God's Word tells us. He has promised to "meet all your needs according to his glorious riches in Christ Jesus" (Phil. 4:19).

A look at the "Proverbs 31 woman" tells us that Scripture does not prohibit a wife from working outside the home or earning money, but rather, her family responsibilities are always to take precedence over outside work, ministry, and activities. It must be noted as well that the godly woman spoken of in Proverbs 31:10-31 was very industrious, but she functioned out of her husband's provision. Since he was "respected at the city gate, where he [took] his seat among the elders of the land," it is to be understood that he was a prosperous man considered capable of governing the city because of the prudent way he had handled his own affairs.

Single moms who must work outside the home can still make choices that enable them to be with their children more, as they rely on the Lord to guide and provide for them. A friend took a lower-paying job that allowed her to start work after her children left for school so that she could be there for them. She then trusted God to provide, and He did.

The husband is also called by God to provide spiritual leadership in the home, which is the third aspect of his role. He may do that by praying with his wife, leading family devotions, or providing opportunities for his wife to attend Bible studies and retreats. But we see that many husbands are not taking up their role as the spiritual leader in any way, and we often pressure them to do so. I remember many years ago when

I was a new believer, Larry finally got these words off his chest: "I can't be what you want me to be." I had pressured him to be like Christian leaders I admired, and that was the wrong message to send.

The point I'm making is that our husbands serve us from a *position* of spiritual leadership, even when they are not fully functioning in it. God will still use them to promote our spiritual growth; He will direct us and speak to us through our husbands. Don't get angry and resentful toward your husband for what he does or fails to do. No one else can interfere with God's will for your life, and that includes your husband. God is still working all things together for your good (Romans 8:28). First Peter 3:1-2 (NASB) tells us, "Wives, in the same way be submissive to your husbands so that, if any of them do not believe the word, they may be won over without talk by the behavior of their wives, when they see the purity and reverence of their lives."

"Without talk"—what a novel idea! This means that Scripture tells us we are not to nag our husbands. Instead, we need to accept them as they are and not try to mold them into a mirror image of us. *Acceptance is the fertile soil in which we all grow.* Walking in the Spirit and being transformed by the renewing of our minds is a full-time job. I find that it is when I don't want to deal with my own attitudes and behaviors that I want to work on someone else's.

If you look up the word *respect* in *The Merriam-Webster Dictionary*, you will see that one of the definitions is "to refrain from interfering with."[2] Respecting our husbands, then, means to stop trying to change them. It's impossible anyway since only God can change a human heart. It is only as we rest in the unconditional love and acceptance that God has for us through Christ that we can be conformed to the image of His Son. As we respect our husbands for the men they are now, we encourage them to become all that God created them to be. God has not "wired" men to be controlled by women; therefore, when we try to control or in any way change them, our husbands will either rebel or become passive—and we will resent them for it. Instead, we are to let God deal with them according to His Word. "The king's heart [one in authority] is in the hand of the Lord; he directs it like a watercourse wherever he pleases" (Prov. 21:1, amplification added).

Just as Christ is to be the "first love" of the church, the husband is to be the "first love" of his wife. Jesus is the Lover of our souls, our King, our Redeemer. Even more, He is our very life. Yet as we learn to love Him more, He will always direct our love towards others. We express our love for Christ by loving others, primarily our own husbands. Just as Christ is to be the "first love" of the church, so the husband is to be the "first love" of his wife. That means he is to come before all *human* relationships and activities—even ministry. He needs to *know* that he is first. One of the ways I check on this is to periodically ask my husband, "Do *you* know that you come first in my life?" He knows I don't mean before the Lord but before all others. If the answer is "no," then I know I've gotten sloppy about my schedule and my attention to him. Do you "hear" what I'm saying? We can't be scheduling meetings (or Bible study) every night of the week, when that's primarily the time our husbands are home. We need to adapt our schedules to theirs and make ourselves available to them.

As wives, we are called to be our husbands' helpmates (Genesis 2:18). If that sounds degrading to you, remember that the Holy Spirit was sent as our "helpmate." As wives are committed to seeing their husbands fulfill their destiny, we will also fulfill our destiny in Christ. Self-sacrifice produces the character of Christ in all of us, both husbands and wives, causing our lives and spiritual gifts to flourish. When a woman is fully surrendered to the will and purposes of God, there is not a man on earth who can keep her from fulfilling her destiny in Christ.

The marriage relationship must come first for another reason: A child-centered home is a home out of order. Children derive their sense of security from the stability of their parents' relationship. When the marriage is modeled after Christ and the church, the children are never neglected, but rather are being raised in a secure environment where they also are loved and respected. When a wife puts her children ahead of her husband, she is disrespecting her husband and over-indulging her children. In effect, she is teaching them not to respect authority.

The Lord is our defender

As we walk in submission to authority, we walk in the light, and the Holy Spirit will show us when our husbands have crossed a boundary and what we should do about it. God commands the husband to treat the wife with gentleness and respect: "Husbands, in the same way be considerate as you live with your wives, and treat them with respect as the weaker partner and as heirs with you of the gracious gift of life, so that nothing will hinder your prayers" (1 Peter 3:7). The Greek word for *hindered* used here is *ekkopto*, which means, "cut off." Please know that harsh or disrespectful husbands will be dealt with by God, and He will be your Defender and Protector. God does not expect us to tolerate unrepentant adultery or any kind of abuse—nothing that is contrary to the Word.

While teaching the *Weatherproof* course, I was informed that one young woman had misunderstood me. She thought that when I told the class they needed to wait on God to change their husbands' hearts, I meant that if the husband is having an affair, the wife should just wait on God—and do nothing. Not true! Just as I stated in a previous chapter concerning physical abuse, God has given us boundaries for our protection. May I suggest a book written by Dr. James Dobson, entitled *Love Must Be Tough*.[3] Dr. Dobson goes into detail about situations that women have allowed to go on in their marriages, all from a warped, non-biblical concept of submission.

According to Matthew 18:15-17, if your husband has been unfaithful to you, you need to confront him. If he repents and is willing to seek counseling for himself and for your relationship, then your marriage can be restored to an even greater level of intimacy than before. But if he refuses to turn away from his sin, that marriage is irreconcilable, and God has not called a wife to submit to her husband under these circumstances. God has instituted church and civil authorities for the protection of women and children. It is the wife's responsibility not to overlook serious transgressions in her husband's behavior, but to seek pastoral counsel for herself and request civil and church intervention when necessary.

Apart from the extremes mentioned above, if the husband is rebelling against God, the solution is not for the wife to rebel against his authority. Tremendous healing and change can occur in a family when the wife begins to respect her husband's authority based on his position, not his performance. Stay under God's umbrella of protection by yielding to your husband's leadership in the day-to-day function of your home, while appealing to Christ to move on your behalf. I have learned that our husbands know when they are not behaving in a way that *deserves* respect. It is exactly in those moments when our faith is tested. We must choose whether we will walk by "sight," as we look at their behavior, or walk by faith as we respond in a way that glorifies God.

How to get from here to there

What shall we do if our marriages are not a true picture of Christ and the church? Here is my deep theological view: Only God can unscramble our eggs! Our human reasoning got us into this mess as we did what we thought was right in our own eyes. Therefore, doing more of the same will not get us out of it. The principles I have laid out in this chapter are boundaries within which the Holy Spirit will give specific, step-by-step instruction tailored to each of our individual situations. He wants you to listen to and obey His voice. But let me remind you that God speaks to us out of the storehouse of His Word in us. Therefore, we must become women of the Word!

Let me tell you about a young friend of mine who came to realize, along with her husband, that she needed to be at home rather than working full time. They have a young daughter who needs a lot of her mom's time and attention. Unfortunately, they came to realize this at a point when they could not financially afford for her to quit her job. I suggested they simply cry out to the Lord together (you can do this alone if your husband doesn't pray with you), confessing the mess they had gotten themselves into by meeting their own needs in their own way. They needed to ask for forgiveness and mercy, and for God to rearrange their circumstances in such a way that the wife would be able to quit her job.

Would you believe that in a little over a year, the young husband was given a position in another state, and the wife had to quit her full-time job here? As it turned out, she only needed a part-time job when she moved and found one with flexible hours that enabled her to be home when her daughter was home before and after school.

I'm not advising you to quit your job; I'm asking you to pray and ask the Lord what adjustments He wants you to make in your lifestyle and how He wants you to get there. "Trust in the Lord with all your heart and lean not on your own understanding; in all your ways acknowledge him, and he will make your path straight" (Prov. 3:5-6 NIV). Cry out to the Lord. Jesus is "the Way" out of our pit. He is able to take our messes and create something new and beautiful. He is so willing to deliver us. Don't believe the lie that your problems can't be solved or that your marriage can't be saved. "With God all things are possible" (Matt. 19:26). All that is required is a willingness to obey and follow His lead; Jesus will supply the power. He will direct our paths; He will calm our fears. Surrender your all to Him.

Always remember that showing respect to your husband heals him of his past wounds, which enables him to love you as God intended. We all come into our marriages with some type of "baggage" from the past, and God uses the marriage relationship to bring healing to those dark places in our souls. Besides, submitting to our husbands (lining up under their position of authority) allows the anointing power of the Living Word, Jesus Christ, to strengthen our families. Let's do things God's way. "Therefore everyone who hears these words of mine and puts them into practice is like a wise man who built his house on the rock. The rain came down, the streams rose and the winds blew and beat against that house, but it did not fall because it had its foundation on the rock" (Matt. 7:24-25).

It is not enough to know what God's Word says; we must put it into practice. Remember that all sin is meeting our own needs in our own way, independently of God.[4] Regarding any adjustments that need to be made in your marriage, begin by embracing the truth of Scripture and repent of rebellion against your God-ordained role. Seek the leading of the Holy Spirit as you choose to devote yourself to your husband out of reverence for Christ, while trusting God to move on your behalf to bring healing to your family for generations.

This chapter's memorization verse is Psalm 81:13-14: "If my people would but listen to me, if [they] would follow my ways, how quickly would I subdue their enemies and turn my hand against their foes." Who is our "foe?" It certainly isn't our husbands, though sometimes we may feel and act as though that were true. Instead, we are told in Ephesians 6:12, "For our struggle is not against flesh and blood, but against the rulers, against the authorities, against the powers of this dark world and against the spiritual forces of evil in the heavenly realms." Satan is out to destroy our families. We must not allow ourselves to be deceived and led away from God's Word. I hear women say that "submission was for those days, not for our day." Not true! Since our marriages are to be modeled after the relationship between Christ and His church, *and that relationship has not changed,* then our marriage roles have not changed. Fight the good fight for the truth and be willing to be a "peculiar people"!

Reflection questions

1. In what ways have you given a higher priority to ministering to those outside your home than you have to your own family? Why have you done so?
2. Some women think they are getting ahead by working. Do you? Is "getting ahead" God's main concern for our lives? If not, what do you see as the consequences of a woman's self-reliance in this area?
3. What changes will you need to make in your beliefs and attitudes for your marriage to come into agreement with the Word of God?

Will you pray with me?

"Gracious heavenly Father, my heart is so full. I pray with all my heart that we—your daughters—would get a revelation that Your Word is true and right, and that we would no longer rely on the world or our own human reasoning, but that we would obey You at all cost. Father, I pray for a special anointing to be upon us so that we would press forward in courage and faith, entrusting our husbands and families to You. We will repent, Lord, we will obey You. In Jesus' name, we pray. Amen."

Memorization verse

Psalm 81:13-14, "If my people would but listen to me, if [they] would follow my ways, how quickly would I subdue their enemies and turn my hand against their foes."

SMALL GROUP DISCUSSION QUESTIONS

Note to discussion leaders: Before proceeding to the discussion questions, it is helpful to begin by asking the women if there was some point in the assigned chapter that they identified with or that was new to them. If time allows, you may also want to discuss the reflection questions listed at the end of the chapter.

1. Even though you may have given "lip service" to the biblical principle of the husband's authority, how has your treatment of your husband shown *you* that you actually reject this principle?
2. A child-centered home is a home out of order. If married, in what ways have you put your children before your husband? Are you meeting your child's needs or are you catering to his or her wants? What is one change you intend to make?
3. Are you struggling to accept any principles presented in this chapter? Can you see where you may be interpreting Scripture based on your personal experiences?

Chapter 12 ❧

It's Not About Us

I'LL BET YOU thought this book was about you. The fact is that God does not heal and restore us, individually and as families, in order for us to live happily ever after behind white picket fences. He has a much higher purpose for us. In order to see a panoramic view of the process I've presented in this book, let's go back to the beginning and do a little review of what I've shared with you.

In Chapter 1, I introduced the concept of strongholds. There are many ways to describe a stronghold, but I see its function in our lives as a strongly held belief or attitude that is contrary to the truth of God's Word, which Satan uses to enslave us to sin. We must understand that our misconceptions (false beliefs) about God the Father have prevented us from turning to Him for the comfort we so desperately need. If we do not turn to Him for comfort, we medicate our pain any way we can, and the world has a multitude of ways for us to do that. God tells us about His comfort in 2 Corinthians 1:3-4: "Praise be to the God and Father of our Lord Jesus Christ, the Father of compassion and the God of all comfort, who comforts us in all our troubles, so that we can comfort those in any trouble with the comfort we ourselves have received from God." This tells us that God the Father is the Source of all comfort; there is no true comfort apart from Him. We are to experience the Father's comfort firsthand, then share it with others, not in order to make others rely on us, but rather, to lead them to experience the Father's comfort for themselves.

Believing that our Father is angry with us will cause us to keep our emotional distance from Him, rather than enjoying an intimate relationship with Him. When I came to faith in Christ, I had such a harsh image of God the Father that I was not able to press into Him. In fact, I just tried to stay out of His way so He wouldn't "nail me." I related to Jesus and to the Holy Spirit, but Jesus' promise that "anyone who has seen me has seen the Father" (John 14:9) didn't get past the filter of my preconceived ideas about the Father.

The precipice called "surrender"

I've recounted for you the time when I could not get up from my living room recliner because I was experiencing a complete emotional meltdown. My husband tells me that I'm over-dramatic (imagine that!), but this is how I pictured it: a murderous enemy was chasing me to the edge of a precipice, and down below were the everlasting arms of God . . . the *Father*, of Whom I was afraid. What a dilemma! I had two choices: throw myself off the precipice and take my chances with the Father, or die a horrible death. A lot of us will not surrender control to the Father until we get that desperate. Have you ever heard that old wives' tale that if you dream you're falling and actually hit bottom in your dream, you'll die? When I mentally cast myself off that precipice, I even had the sensation of falling, and I thought I would die. Instead, it seemed as though I landed in a feathered nest.

It wasn't that God had merely *allowed* certain circumstances in my life. God did for me what I could not do for myself. When we are not emotionally able to "go there," when there is some misconception that's keeping us from intimacy with the Father, He will *orchestrate* the events of our lives in such a way that we are compelled to leap off that precipice called "surrender." That's what He did for me: my heavenly Father caught me and brought me into a relationship with Him that I did not know existed. If we don't have that intimate relationship with Him, we'll live self-reliant rather than God-dependent lives. And, unfortunately, many in the church—yes, members of the body of Christ—are living self-reliant lives.

We tear down a stronghold by taking these false beliefs captive, bringing them into submission to the Word of God. Now let's continue to do that as we look at Romans 4:23-25, which is speaking of Abraham's faith: "The words 'it was credited to him' were written not for him alone, but also for us, to whom God will credit righteousness—for us who believe in him who raised Jesus our Lord from the dead. He was delivered over to death for our sins and was raised to life for our justification." The belief that God the Father cannot be pleased with us because of our sin reveals that we have not embraced the truth that we have been placed into Christ and credited with His righteousness.

Do you recall the analogy of the credit account? We have been charged with the enormous debt of our sin. "For the wages of sin is death" (Rom. 6:23), and that is what we earned and deserve. But by His death and resurrection, Christ paid our debt, bringing it to a zero balance and giving us a clean slate. Amazingly, He also credited our account with His infinite righteousness, assuring us of eternal right standing with God the Father. Jesus Christ took all of our sin upon Himself and gave us His righteousness, so that when the Father looks at you (and me), He sees the righteousness of Jesus Christ. Therefore, for those who received Christ as Savior, all of the Father's righteous anger over our sins was poured out on Christ at the cross, and we are free to enjoy an intimate relationship with the Father.

> Since we have now been justified by his blood, how much more shall we be saved from God's wrath through him! For if, when we were God's enemies, we were reconciled to him through the death of his Son, how much more, having been reconciled, shall we be saved through his life! Not only is this so, but we also rejoice in God through our Lord Jesus Christ, through whom we have now received reconciliation.
>
> —Rom. 5:9-11

Reconciliation is peace with God and right standing with God through Jesus Christ our Lord. Have we forgotten why Jesus came? He came to bring us into relationship with our heavenly Father.

Cast your cares upon Him

In the sacred journey we're on—from the self-centered life based on human reasoning to the life that is fully surrendered to the will and purposes of God—God doesn't immediately show us all the changes He intends to bring about in our lives. He knows we're a work in progress, and He's patient because He knows that the process is the point: that's how we come to know Him.

One of the problem areas that the Lord has had to work on in my life is my tendency to be too serious with an over-developed sense of responsibility. Survival is serious business, and for years I put all my energy into surviving, not trusting God to take care of me. However His Word tells us to "cast all your anxiety [cares] upon him because he cares for you" (1 Peter 5:7). Why didn't I let Him do what He does best—and relax? I prayed, "More, Lord. I've cast so much on You already, but I see that there's more 'casting' that I need to do." What a waste! So caught up with arranging other people's lives to protect myself, I was not living my own life.

One of the things I sacrificed in the process was joyful living, and that's too high a price to pay. By God's grace and mercy, I'm experiencing more and more freedom from that mindset every day. Joy is the fruit of the Spirit (Galatians 5:22) produced in us if we are willing to let go of control. That's a scary thought for many of us. But do you know what's even scarier? Living a life without J-O-Y!

> When the Lord brought back the captives to Zion,
> we were like men who dreamed.
> Our mouths were filled with laughter,
> our tongues with songs of joy.
> Then it was said among the nations,
> "The Lord has done great things for them."
> The Lord has done great things for us,
> and we are filled with joy.
>
> —Ps. 126:1-3

Believers are receivers, not performers

We can, and must, move from a performance-based to a love-based relationship with our heavenly Father. The pressure is off—what a relief! We don't have to perform to receive the Father's love—we simply receive it. Everything good in our lives comes from God the Father, through the finished work of Jesus Christ, by the power of the Holy Spirit. The apostle Peter tells us: "His [Jesus'] divine power has given us everything we need for life and godliness through our knowledge of him who called us by his own glory and goodness" (2 Peter 1:3). All of our needs are met in Christ: "everything we need for life and godliness." What else is there? He has accomplished everything. And how do we receive everything we need? "Through our knowledge of Him. . . ." And how do we know Him? Jesus is the Living Word, and we know Him through the written Word, the Scriptures, by the power of the Holy Spirit. "Through these [his own glory and goodness] he has given us his very great and precious promises, so that through them [his promises] you may participate in the divine nature and escape the corruption in the world caused by evil desires" (2 Peter 1:4, amplification added).

Please recall from Chapters 6 and 7, when we studied our identity in Christ, that we no longer have a "sin nature." We have been given a new nature through our union with Christ, so that we can participate in *His* divine nature. We are no longer compelled to sin; when we sin, it is because we choose to walk in the flesh, rather than according to the Spirit. Through the promised Holy Spirit, we can live holy (though imperfect) lives, rather than be corrupted, as the world is, by evil desires. Peter goes on to tell us:

> For this very reason, make every effort to add to your faith goodness; and to goodness, knowledge; and to knowledge, self-control; and to self-control, perseverance; and to perseverance, godliness; and to godliness, brotherly kindness; and to brotherly kindness, love. For, if you possess these qualities in increasing measure, they will keep you from being ineffective and unproductive in your knowledge of our Lord Jesus Christ. But if anyone does not have them, he is nearsighted and blind, and has forgotten that he has been cleansed from his past sins.
> —2 Peter 1:5-9

I hope you can see from that entire passage that the point is not for us to try harder in our human effort. We are commanded to bring to mind the truth that we have been cleansed from our past sins, to remember that we have been placed into Christ and credited with His righteousness. As we read and believe the promises of the Word of

God, our faith is increased, and that is the starting point. Then we are told to "add to our faith. . . ." In order for that to happen, we need to "make every effort" to study and meditate on the Word of God, to seek the knowledge of Christ through His Word, so that as we spend time with Him, we will become like Him. If we don't, we will find ourselves "ineffective and unproductive in our knowledge" of Him. The more time we spend in His Word, the more these qualities will be produced in us. The more these qualities are produced in us (as we walk under the control of the Holy Spirit), the more productive we will be in our knowledge of Him . . . from glory to glory! We may say that we want to grow spiritually, but if we do not invest our time and effort in the study of God's Word, we can't know Him and His ways.

We do nothing in our own power. Even the good works we are to do have already been prepared—by God Himself. They are not done through human effort; therefore, the pressure is not on us to perform but simply to trust and obey. "For we are God's workmanship, created in Christ Jesus to do good works, which God prepared in advance for us to do" (Eph. 2:10). We are to receive these good works and do them in the power of the Holy Spirit so that they are God's work from beginning to end. Then who gets the glory? God gets the glory!

Let's see what God is doing

Scripture teaches us that instead of doing a good work of our own choosing and then asking God to bless it, we are to first "see" what God is doing, receive it by faith, and carry it out in the power of the Holy Spirit. "Where there is no vision, the people perish" (Prov. 29:18 KJV). In C. I. Scofield's notes on this verse, he states, "The Hebrew word rendered 'vision' is not the ordinary word for something seen. Rather, it indicates a revelation from God, such as the visions that the prophets saw."[1] He is not speaking of seeing something with our physical sight, but rather that it is revealed to us in our spirits.

Sometimes God shows us a picture of what He is doing, or it may simply be a "knowing" or understanding. To understand what I mean by this, let's look at John 5:19 to see how Jesus explained it: "Jesus gave them this answer: 'I tell you the truth, the Son can do nothing by himself; he can do only what he sees his Father doing, because whatever the

Father does the Son also does." Jesus is fully God and fully man. In His humanity, He modeled for us what it means to be God-dependent. He spent time alone with His Father, and in that intimate relationship with Him, the Father revealed to Jesus the good works He was to do; then Jesus did them in the power of the Holy Spirit, just as we are to do.

"Seeing," which is revelation, comes from intimacy with God. Even Jesus said that He could only do what He *saw* the Father doing. He is showing us a principle here: We must spend "alone" time with our heavenly Father in childlike adoration. Early one morning, with darkness surrounding me, I began listening to worship music and thinking about God the Father. I became so caught up in the words of the song, which spoke of His love for me, that I wanted to dance before Him. Even though I was fifty-three years old at the time, I "saw" myself as a three-year-old child dancing before her Daddy—in a pink tutu, pink leotards, and a diamond tiara! Actually, I didn't dance—I twirled. I twirled in my tutu! Over and over again, until I was dizzy, this grandmother twirled in her living room, losing her balance and falling down, all the while giggling like a three-year-old child. And in my heart, I heard my heavenly Father laughing with me! Not everyone had that kind of sweet and tender experience with their earthly father, but we can each have uniquely intimate experiences with God that will be meaningful to us. We *must* come to know that God absolutely delights in us, that He enjoys us, all because of what Christ has done on our behalf. Then the Father will give us the knowledge and the power to do His will.

The anointed works of God

John Wesley defined the anointing as "capacitating gifts and commissioned authority"[2] (the work of the Holy Spirit). But how can we walk in spiritual authority if we are not walking *under* spiritual authority? We cannot. Remember the centurion who requested that Jesus heal his beloved servant? In Luke 7:6b-9, we are told that he sent word to Jesus,

> "Lord, don't trouble yourself, for I do not deserve to have you come under my roof. That is why I did not even consider myself worthy to

come to you. But say the word, and my servant will be healed. For I myself am a man under authority, with soldiers under me. I tell this one, 'Go,' and he goes; and that one, 'Come,' and he comes. I say to my servant, 'Do this,' and he does it." When Jesus heard this, he was amazed at him, and turning to the crowd following him, he said, "I tell you, I have not found such great faith even in Israel."

When we place ourselves under all God-ordained authority, we are operating out of our faith in God. We are submitting to God and, therefore, can resist the devil by standing firm in our faith (1 Peter 5:9), forcing the devil to flee according to God's Word (James 4:7). It is by submitting to authority in all areas of our lives, beginning in our homes, that God provides the spiritual covering of protection against the demonic realm. I want to remind you of the umbrella of protection, which is a picture of authority, with a shaft of light coming down from under that umbrella. Why? Authority is God's will; therefore, when we are submitting to authority we are walking in the light. Remember also that rebellion is Satan's domain and is pictured as spiritual darkness outside the perimeter of the umbrella.

Staying under authority is obviously not the only protection we have. We are also called to put on the full armor of God (Ephesians 6:11). We are in a spiritual battle, and we are not to be passive. The enemy doesn't come under the umbrella of authority to attack us; he shoots "flaming arrows" at us. When we put on the full armor of God, we "take up the shield of faith by which [we] can extinguish all the flaming arrows of the evil one" (verse 16). In our other hand, we have "the sword of the Spirit, which is the word of God" (verse 17). We do indeed have many divine weapons, but they won't do us any good if we do not first stay under authority.

The Lord brings us under our husbands' position of authority so that when we move into ministry, we will do so in the anointing and the power of the Holy Spirit, without allowing Satan to bring destruction to our homes. Every believer is anointed to do the good works that God prepared in advance for us to do. Are we anointed to do anything else? No . . . how could we be? If the anointing is God's power to accomplish God's purposes, He is not going to anoint anything that He has not prepared in advance for us to do. These good works are not of our choosing; they are God's. We have seen, through Scripture, the biblical mandate to us as women to put our husbands before all other human relationships and activities and to submit to their leadership. That means we are anointed to do this. It also means that we do not have the option of bypassing that good work in order to do other "good works." God has not prepared other good works that will compete with His stated priority in our marriages. That's one way we can know if some ministry or activity is God's will for us. With that in mind, let's see what God's Word has to say about the responsibilities of the husband, as we consider First Timothy 3:1-5. This passage defines the criteria for choosing an overseer in the church (a bishop, pastor, elder):

> Here is a trustworthy saying: If anyone sets his heart on being an overseer, he desires a noble task. Now the overseer must be above reproach, the husband of but one wife, temperate, self-controlled, respectable, hospitable, able to teach, not given to drunkenness, not violent but gentle, not quarrelsome, not a lover of money.
>
> —vv. 1-3

Verse 2 tells us that he is to be the husband of one wife (Greek *gune* = woman), so we are speaking of men here. Then in verses 4-5, we're told: "He must manage his own family well and see that his children obey him with proper respect. (If anyone does not know how to manage his own family, how can he take care of God's church?)" This passage tells us that the husband is responsible before God for the condition of his family. A man is also expected to "manage his own family well" as the criteria for overseeing the church. The Greek word for *manage* (*proistemi*) means "to superintend, preside over; to be a protector or guardian." The picture here is of a shepherd, tenderly leading and caring for his flock, as modeled by the Good Shepherd Himself.

Scripture speaks of the woman's responsibilities, in Titus 2:3-5:

> Likewise, teach the older women to be reverent in the way they live, not to be slanderers or addicted to much wine, but to teach what is good. Then they can train the younger women to love their husbands and children, to be self-controlled and pure, to be busy at home, to be kind, and to be subject to their husbands, so that no one will malign the word of God.

159

To be "busy at home" (*oikouros*) means "caring for the house, taking care of household affairs," but also means "the (watch or) keeper of the house." The last part of the Greek word *ouros* means "a guard." The sense is that we are the "watchmen on the wall," an Old Testament role needed to protect the city. Yes, it is keeping an orderly home and providing nurturing care for our families, but this is a position of spiritual warfare that God has given us—that sensitivity and attentiveness to warn our husbands when we are alerted that something is wrong, perhaps with one of our children. That is part of our essential function in the family.

How cunning of Satan to lure women away from their homes so that no one is on guard to warn when danger is approaching.

Christ is the cornerstone of the church, and yes, we are individually the living stones that make up the church, but God has chosen to join us together as families. As the family goes, so goes the church. As Satan seeks to "kill, steal, and destroy" (John 10:10), we see his attack against the body of Christ manifesting in the marriages and families within the church. To counter his attacks, it is essential that we understand our high calling, as God has given women this powerful and influential position on behalf of our families.

Ministry begins at home but does not end there

Jesus quoted from Isaiah 61:1 when He began His ministry as recorded in Luke 4. Just as Christ applied this passage to Himself when He began His ministry, I realized that because I had been placed into union with Christ, the Anointed One, the Spirit of the Sovereign Lord is on *me—and you*. We can receive this truth for ourselves: "The Spirit of the Sovereign Lord is on [us] for He has anointed [us] to preach good news to the poor, to bind up the brokenhearted, to proclaim freedom for the captives and release from darkness for the prisoners." Let's now look to God's Word to summarize our pilgrimage, as He calls us to ministry:

> For Christ's love compels us, because we are all convinced that one died for all, and therefore all died. And he died for all, that those who live should no longer live for themselves but for him who died for them and was raised again. So from now on we regard no one from a worldly point of view. Though we once regarded Christ in this way,

160

we do so no longer. Therefore, if anyone is in Christ, he is a new creation; the old has gone, the new has come! All this is from God, who reconciled us to himself through Christ and gave us the ministry of reconciliation: that God was reconciling the world to himself in Christ, not counting men's sins against them. And he has committed to us the message of reconciliation.

—2 Cor. 5:14-19

You have been reminded of what Christ has accomplished on your behalf: peace and right standing with God the Father and the anointing power of the Holy Spirit. It took me all these years to understand that Jesus came to bring me into that reconciled relationship with the Father. He loves us! He delights in us! He deals with our behavior, but He does so in love. Yet our awareness of God's presence, power, and love for us does not cause us to be self-absorbed and oblivious of our surroundings. In fact, we have a heightened awareness of the needs of others.

We are called to the "ministry of reconciliation," declaring to a lost and dying world that they can be reconciled with God the Father, through faith in His Son, Jesus Christ. This ministry is more than mere words; this is loving action. When we truly begin to comprehend the Father's unconditional love and tenderness towards us, and what Christ has done to provide it all for us, we are *compelled* to share that message of reconciliation—in word and deed. The Lord will give us opportunities to share the Good News—perhaps over a cup of coffee with a neighbor—in ways that are so simple, yet so powerful when the Holy Spirit is in charge.

This is just the beginning

Do you recall the image the Lord gave me of the gnarly tree—a picture of me being so deeply rooted and grounded in the Word of God that I would not be moved by the storms of life? That image is not for me alone, I know, but is for every one of us. I now know why! The Lord tells us in Isaiah 61:3, "They will be called oaks of righteousness, a planting of the Lord for the display of his splendor." That gnarly old tree was an oak of righteousness, beautiful in the sight of the Lord, for the display of *HIS* splendor. Awesome!

God is calling His beloved daughters to serve Him in a *worldwide, counter-cultural women's movement*, to "rebuild the ancient ruins and restore the places long devastated; [to] renew the ruined cities that have been devastated for generations" (Isa. 61:4). My prayer for you, my friend, is that you would walk in God's ways, know Him through a loving relationship, and bring Him glory.

Love, Donna

Reflection questions

1. Have you realized that your fear of God the Father, which is the result of misconceptions about Him, is a root cause for some of the problems in your life? Will you pray, asking Him to correct your beliefs about Him?
2. Can you recall a time of intimacy with God the Father, where you experienced His unconditional and tenderhearted love for you? If you have not, you can cry out to Him right now, for He desires this even more than you do.

Will you pray with me?

I hope you will join with me, and with your many sisters in Christ who have been on this sacred journey with us, as we pray for a renewed dedication of our lives.

"Lord God, I confess that I have gone my own way and leaned upon my own understanding. I have allowed the world to lure me away from obedience and surrender to You, and I have allowed Satan to deceive me in many ways. But I trust in Your mercy and in Your power to enable me to live the life You've called me to live "in Christ." I ask You, Father, in the name of the Lord Jesus Christ, and by the power of His blood, to 'turn my eyes away from worthless things; renew my life according to Your Word' (Ps. 119:37). Amen."

Memorization verse

Ps. 119:37, "Turn my eyes away from worthless things; renew my life according to your word."

This is your final memorization verse. Write it on your heart and keep it with you at all times. Remember that God always answers "yes" to a prayer that lines up with His will.

SMALL GROUP DISCUSSION QUESTIONS

Note to discussion leaders: This section has been included for groups allowing time or an additional session for discussion and review of Chapter 12. Before proceeding to the discussion questions, it is helpful to begin by asking the women if there was some point in the assigned chapter that they identified with or that was new to them. If time allows, you may also want to discuss the reflection questions listed at the end of the chapter.

1. Have you been a "performer" in your Christian life? Are you ready to step back and wait for the Lord to reveal to you the good works He has prepared in advance for you to do (Eph. 2:10)? Keep in mind that there may be a period of time where you aren't "doing" anything. Why do you think you would be uncomfortable with that?
2. Have you become aware that you don't spend a lot of conscious thought about God throughout your day? We become so busy that our thoughts become caught up with the details of life. In order to improve in this area, honestly discuss what your thoughts focus on for much of the day.
3. What have you learned from God's Word that has most changed your perception of how God sees you and the purpose He has for your life?

Endnotes

Introduction

1. Franklin Graham, *Rebel With A Cause* (Nashville: Nelson Publishing, 1995), 313. Used by permission.
2. Klyne Snodgrass, *Ephesians: The NIV Application Commentary* (Grand Rapids: Zondervan, 1996), 342.

Chapter 1—The Lives We Construct

1. International Bible Society, *The NIV Study Bible,* (Grand Rapids: Zondervan, 1995), 971.
2. Dr. Neil T. Anderson, *Victory Over the Darkness,* 28. Copyright © 1990 by Regal Books, Ventura, CA 93003. Used by permission. Recommended reading.
3. Charles R. Solomon, *The Ins and Out of Rejection* (Sevierville, TN: Solomon Publications, 1991), 125.
4. Anderson, *Victory,* 79.
5. "By permission. From *The Merriam-Webster Dictionary* ©2004 by Merriam-Webster®, Incorporated. ("http://www.merriam-webster. com)/"
6. Anderson, *Victory,* 28.
7. Anderson, *Victory,* 43.

Chapter 2—The Destruction Caused by Bitterness

1. Bill Gothard, *How to Tear Down the Stronghold of Bitterness* © 1992 by IBLP, 3. Used by permission. Ideas behind the material used in this chapter were influenced by Mr. Gothard's teaching.
2. Gothard, *Bitterness,* 5.
3. *Merriam-Webster® Dictionary* ©2004.
4. ibid.
5. ibid.
6. ibid.

Chapter 3—Experiencing God's Mercy

1. *Merriam-Webster® Dictionary* © 2004.
2. Snodgrass, *Ephesians,* 56.
3. Glenda Revell, *Glenda's Story: Led By Grace* (Lincoln, NE: Gateway to Joy, 1994), 98.
4. *Merriam-Webster® Dictionary* ©2004.
5. ibid.

Chapter 4—Tearing Down a Stronghold of Self-Deception (Part 1)

1. Anderson, *Victory,* 28.

Chapter 5—Tearing Down a Stronghold of Self-Deception (Part 2)

1. *Merriam-Webster® Dictionary* ©2004
2. Diane Passno, *Feminism: Mystique or Mistake?* (Wheaton, IL: Tyndale House Publishers, 2000), 27. Used by permission.
3. Passno, *Feminism,* 102.
4. Author unknown.
5. Anderson, *Victory,* 79.
6. Dr. Rockwell Dillaman, unpublished sermon: *Ministering the Cross of Jesus Christ* (Allegheny Center Alliance Church, Pittsburgh, PA), 3. Used by permission.
7. Dillaman, *Ministering the Cross,* 2.

8. All quotations in this prayer, other than Scripture, are taken from the Bible tract, *How I Learned to Pray for the Lost,* by Back to the Bible. Reprinted by permission from the *Alliance Witness.*

Chapter 6—A Solid Foundation—Our Identity in Christ (Part 1)

1. Anderson, *Victory,* 18.
2. Anderson, *Victory,* 43.
3. Anderson, *Victory,* 18.
4. Snodgrass, *Ephesians,* 56.
5. Snodgrass, *Ephesians,* 49.
6. Alan F. Johnson, *Everyman's Bible Commentary: Romans* (Chicago: Moody Press, 1974), 75.

Chapter 7—A Solid Foundation—Our Identity in Christ (Part 2)

1. Snodgrass, *Ephesians,* 56.
2. Anderson, *Victory,* 43.
3. Anderson, *Victory,* 76
4. Anderson, *Victory,* 45.
5. Johnson, *Romans,* 115.
6. Johnson, *Romans,* 75.

Chapter 8—The Person and Work of the Holy Spirit

1. David Wilkerson, *Hungry For More of Jesus: Experiencing His Presence in These Troubled Times* (Grand Rapids, MI: Chosen Books, 1992), 102.
2. C. I. Scofield (Ed). *The New Scofield Reference Bible: Authorized King James Version* (New York: Oxford University Press, 1967), 1371.
3. John F. Walvoord, *The Revelation of Jesus Christ* (Chicago: Moody Press, 1966), 333.
4. Johnson, *Romans,* 220.

Chapter 9—Families in Crisis—A Home Out of Order

1. NIV Study Bible, 971.
2. Anderson, *Victory,* 28.

3. NIV Study Bible, 114-115.
4. NIV Study Bible, 781.
5. John Wesley, *Commentary on Ephesians 5*. John Wesley's Explanatory Notes on the Whole Bible. <http://bible.crosswalk.com/Commentaries/WesleysExplanatoryNotes/wes.cgi?book=eph&chapter=005>. 1765. Public domain.
6. Mike Quarles, former Co-Director of Freedom In Christ Ministry with his wife, Julia, made this statement in their *Freedom From Addiction Workshop*.

Chapter 10—God's Design for Marriage

1. John MacArthur, Jr., *Family Feuding, How to End It: Study notes on Ephesians 5:21-6:4* (Panorama City, CA: Word of Grace Communications, 1981), 13.
2. Snodgrass, *Ephesians*, 295.
3. Author unknown.
4. John Wesley, *Commentary on Isaiah 61*. John Wesley's Explanatory Notes on the Whole Bible. <http://bible.crosswalk.com/Commentaries/WesleysExplanatoryNotes/wes.cgi?book=isa&chapter=061>.1754. Public domain.
5. *Amplified Bible, New Testament* © 1987. LaHabre, CA: The Lockman Foundation
6. *Merriam-Webster® Dictionary* © 2004
7. ibid.
8. ibid.
9. ibid.
10. ibid.
11. ibid.
12. ibid.
13. ibid.

Chapter 11—Ministry Begins at Home

1. Wesley, *Ephesians 5*.
2. *Merriam-Webster® Dictionary* © 2004.

3. Dr. James Dobson, *Love Must Be Tough* (Nashville, TN: Word Book Publishing, 1983). Recommended reading.
4. Anderson, *Victory,* 28.

Chapter 12—It's Not About Us

1. Scofield, 693.
2. Wesley, *Isaiah 61.*

To order additional copies of this book,
please visit www.redemption-press.com
Also available on Amazon.com and BarnesandNoble.com
Or by calling toll free (844) 273-3336

CPSIA information can be obtained
at www.ICGtesting.com
Printed in the USA
BVHW01s1721070218
507513BV00031B/1440/P